浙江省普通高校“十三五”新形态教材
宁波工程学院教材出版资助

中国文化简明教程

A Brief Introduction to Chinese Culture

莫群俐 主编

浙江工商大學出版社
ZHEJIANG GONGSHANG UNIVERSITY PRESS
·杭州·

图书在版编目(CIP)数据

中国文化简明教程 = A Brief Introduction to Chinese Culture：英文、中文 / 莫群俐主编．—杭州：浙江工商大学出版社，2021.5

ISBN 978-7-5178-4205-7

Ⅰ．①中… Ⅱ．①莫… Ⅲ．①汉语—对外汉语教学—教材—汉、英 ②中华文化—介绍—汉、英 Ⅳ．①H195.4 ②K203

中国版本图书馆 CIP 数据核字(2020)第251718号

中国文化简明教程（A Brief Introduction to Chinese Culture）

ZHONGGUO WENHUA JIANMING JIAOCHENG

莫群俐 主编

责任编辑 姚 媛

封面设计 叶泽雯

责任印制 包建辉

出版发行 浙江工商大学出版社

（杭州市教工路198号 邮政编码310012）

（E-mail:zjgsupress@163.com）

（网址:http://www.zjgsupress.com）

电话:0571-88904980,88831806(传真)

排　　版 杭州朝曦图文设计有限公司

印　　刷 广东虎彩云印刷有限公司绍兴分公司

开　　本 787 mm×1092 mm 1/16

印　　张 11

字　　数 220千

版 印 次 2021年5月第1版 2021年5月第1次印刷

书　　号 ISBN 978-7-5178-4205-7

定　　价 42.00元

Foreword

On October 18th, 2017, in the report of the 19th National Congress of the Communist Party of China (CPC), President Xi Jinping metioned Chinese culture many times, and he pointed out that "we will improve our capacity for engaging in international communication so as to tell China's stories well, present a true, multi-dimensional, and panoramic view of China, and enhance our country's cultural soft power." And Xi Jinping stressed that "with this we will see that Chinese culture maintains its appeal and evolves with the times."

With the increase of China's international influence, coupled with the Belt and Road Initiative, more and more foreigners come to China for traveling, studying, and living, which provides an opportunity for spreading traditional Chinese culture. Among them, the overseas students in colleges and universities are the most ideal force.

Under such circumstances, *A Brief Introduction to Chinese Culture*, mainly for overseas students in China, therefore, comes into being.

Like other cultures in the world, Chinese culture is changing continually. With the strenuous work of the whole nation, China has witnessed fundamental changes in every field. People are enjoying the peace and harmony in economy, culture and education, daily life, and entertainment and leisure. Our country's construction and development are changing with each passing day, and people's thoughts, views, and lifestyles have also undergone great changes.

Accordingly, from making plans to hatching plots, and from working out schemes to carrying out the writings, the author has been diligent and conscientious to provide readers with a rich and colorful introduction of an encyclopedic manner in two texts, including not only traditional Chinese culture, but also China's current reform and opening-up policy, urban and rural life, etc. in the first part of each chapter. And sure enough, the new and creative series will bring brand new feelings and experiences to all readers.

In the second part of each chapter, "Chinese Eyes on the World" is to tell about a relevant theme of the world in the eyes of Chinese people, which will undoubtedly give readers a new aspect to understand Chinese people.

Culture course is important for learners to understand and master the differences and communication between different cultures. Therefore, the last part of each chapter of this book includes rich cultural exchange practices so that the use of this textbook in the classroom will achieve the student-centered purpose of capacity building, which refers to emphasizing teamwork rather than individual work, solving problems on their own and making independent decisions under imperfect conditions so as to constantly improve their decision-making abilities, and applying their knowledge to practice by visualizing and materializing abstract theories.

This textbook is not only suitable for international students in China for their culture courses, but also good for college English extension courses and elective courses for majors of English, foreign trade, foreign affairs, tourism, Chinese as a foreign language, etc. It can be used as a college English teacher's reference book. It can also unveil the mysteries of China for all of the foreigners who are interested in Chinese culture.

The original intent of compiling this textbook is to promote Chinese culture, enrich English teaching materials, and foster English teaching reform. We apologize for the insufficient information in some aspects due to lack of resources. We intend to show every respect for intellectual property rights, but we hope our pleading of the permission to use these materials for the purpose of letting more foreign friends know China better will receive kind and generous consideration. Last but not least, many thanks to the School of Economics and Management in Ningbo University of Technology for its monographs fund support.

前　言

2017年10月18日，习近平在中国共产党第十九次全国代表大会上的报告里多次提到中华文化，习近平强调要“推进国际传播能力建设，讲好中国故事，展现真实、立体、全面的中国，提高国家文化软实力”，要“让中华文化展现出永久魅力和时代风采”。

随着我国国际影响力的日渐增强，以及“一带一路”倡议的推进，越来越多的外国人来华旅游、留学、居住，这为传播中国传统文化提供了契机。而在来华群体中，高校留学生群体是最为理想的传播中国传统文化之主力军。

在这种形势下，我们编写了《中国文化简明教程》，主要供来华的留学生使用。

与世界上其他文化一样，中国文化也在不断变化。在中国人民的辛勤努力下，中国在各个方面都发生了翻天覆地的变化。从经济、文化和教育，到生活、娱乐和休闲，人们都在尽情地享受着和平与和谐。国家的建设和发展日新月异，人们的思想观念和生活方式也有了很大的变化。

因此，《中国文化简明教程》从策划到构思，从设计到编写，都是力求创造性地介绍中国的传统文化，同时也把中国当今的改革开放、城乡生活等以简洁流畅的语言在每一章的第一部分的两篇文章中加以叙述。通过本部分的阅读，读者可以对中国文化有个多方面的基本了解。

在每一章的第二部分编排了“中国人看世界”，讲述中国人眼中的某一个相关主题，这无疑给广大读者了解中国人提供了一个全新的视角。

文化课程是学习者了解和掌握文化差异和跨文化交际的一门重要课程。因此，本书在每一章的最后一部分设计了丰富的文化交流实践内容，从而使该教材在课堂上达到以学生为主，着眼于其能力培养的目的：强调团队合作，而非个体单干；引导学生独立解决问题，并在不圆满的条件下做出自己独立的决策，从而不断提高决策能力，使得抽象的理论形象化、具体化，做到学以致用。

本书不仅可供来华留学生的文化课程使用，也可供高等学校大学英语拓展课程，如英语、外贸、外事、旅游、对外汉语等专业的选修课程使用，也可作为高校英语教师的参考资料，还可以为所有对中国文化感兴趣的外国友人揭开中国的神秘面纱。

我们编写本书的初衷是弘扬中华民族文化，丰富英语教材建设，促进英语教学改革。由于文化研究涉及面广，一些素材选自国内外有关中国的出版物或网络资料，在此向原作者表示衷心的感谢。最后，也衷心感谢宁波工程学院经济与管理学院学术专著基金的支持。由于编者水平有限，书中错漏之处在所难免，欢迎读者批评指正。

Contents

Chapter 1 Holidays and Festivals

Text Reading

Micro-video

Spring Festival

◎ Text A

Spring Festival—the Biggest Festival in China

The Spring Festival, also known as the Chinese Lunar New Year, which falls in late January or early February according to the Gregorian calendar, is the most important festival for the Chinese as it is an occasion for reunion with family and friends. Particularly, people working away from their hometown hope to have a Reunion Dinner with family on the Lunar New Year's Eve.

Hundreds of millions of Chinese people are on journey as the Spring Festival travel season begins. Therefore, it has created enormous pressure on China's transportation sector. Transportation around the Spring Festival, called Spring Travel, is an annual test on China's transportation system. The National Railway Administration and the National Development and Reform Commission usually issue circulars during the period, demanding that coordination mechanisms be established among transportation departments, local authorities, and police, and that countermeasures be made in place in case of emergencies to ensure efficiency and to achieve success during the peak travel season.

Micro-video

Spring Travel

It is said that only those who have taken long-distance trains during the Spring Festival travel rush can really understand China.

Since the Spring Festival is known as the most important traditional festival in China, many customs accompany the Spring Festival, some of which are still followed today, even though some have weakened.

Before the lunar new year comes, people clean the indoors and outdoors completely as well as their clothes, bedclothes, and all utensils. Before the day of the lunar new year, people put "*Fu*" Character (meaning blessing) and couplets in red on the door, and people believe doing these will bring their family happiness and auspiciousness.

At the Spring Festival's Eve, the whole family will happily have the Reunion Dinner. Some families will go to the restaurant to have the Reunion Dinner. The meal is more luxurious than usual. After the dinner, the whole family will sit together, chatting and watching TV.

In China, the most traditional and popular Spring Festival food is dumpling, which looks like the half moon and usually with vegetables and meat mixed in it. The Chinese name of dumpling is "*jiaozi.*" "*Jiao*" means "cross," and "*zi*" is Chinese traditional time representing "24: 00," so the Chinese term "*jiaozi*" means "cross 24: 00," just the dividing point of last year and next year. So when it comes to 24:00, every family begins eating dumplings in Chinese tradition.

The Spring Festival is also the happiest time for children, because they can receive red packets containing money as a gift from the elder. During the Spring Festival, any unfortunate words cannot be heard because they will make people upset and unhappy.

On the New Year's Eve, people usually watch the CCTV's Spring Festival Gala at home. At the same time massive blessing messages are sent to friends and relatives. The elders will give the younger generation(s) a big red envelope with money in it, and the young will say many blessings, such as:

Best wishes for the New Year!

May you come into a good fortune!

I wish you longevity and health!

Extended Reading

Daily Customs of Spring Festival

Burning fireworks was once the most typical custom during the Spring Festival. People thought the spluttering sound could help drive away evil spirits. However, such an activity has been completely or partially forbidden in big cities once the government took factors like security, noise, and pollution into consideration.

In fact, Spring Festival refers to a period of time, lasting from the evening preceding the first day of the lunar new year to the fifteenth day. In the past, from the first day of the year to the fifteenth, people would pay New Year's visit to their relatives and friends. Nowadays, more and more people do that by phone, text message, and WeChat.

Micro-video

Lantern Festival & Riddles

The fifteenth day is the last day of the Spring Festival, known as the Lantern Festival. On this day, people go along the street to watch lanterns and children light their own small lanterns for some fun. The biggest and most beautiful lantern is the dragon lantern, which looks like a flying Chinese dragon held by several young guys.

The traditional food for the Lantern Festival is rice glue ball, called *yuanxiao*, which is a flavor ball with filling in it, for example, peanut, sesame, jam, etc. The rice glue ball's shape is just like the full moon appearing in the sky, which symbolizes reunion. This kind of dessert is especially welcomed by children.

The traditional activity of the Lantern Festival is to guess riddles on the lanterns. Usually on the night of the Lantern Festival, in the streets, alleys, and courtyards, people will see lanterns with riddles written on them, called lantern riddles, and those who figure out the answer can receive small presents and be happy for their own intelligence.

The Lantern Festival is the last day of the Spring Festival. After this day, people will admit that the Spring Festival is over and everyone should settle down to work.

春节——中国最隆重的节日

春节，即中国农历新年，通常在公历1月末或2月初。它是中国人最重要的节日，是家人及亲朋好友团聚的日子。在外地工作的人们尤其盼望赶回家中与家人一起吃年夜饭。

春节期间，数以亿计的中国人都在旅途中奔波，因此，它给中国的交通造成了巨大的压力。中国人将春节前后一段时间的运输业务简称为“春运”，它是对中国交通运输系统的年度考验。国家铁路局和国家发改委在此期间会下发各类通知，要求运输部门、地方各级部门、公安部门建立协调机制，制定各种措施以应对紧急情况的发生，确保运输效率，保证人流高峰季节的运输得以顺利完成。

有这样一种说法：只有在春运期间坐过长途火车的人，才能真正了解中国。

春节是公认的中国最重要的传统节日，相应地就有许多习俗，虽然有些已渐淡化，但其中一些仍延续至今。

在新的一年到来之前，人们对室内和室外进行大扫除，对衣服、床上用品和所有厨具也都清洁一番。新年第一天，人们在门上贴上"福"字和红红的对联，他们认为这样做新的一年会给家里人带来好运。

在除夕，全家人一起开心地吃团圆饭。一些家庭会去饭店吃团圆饭。这顿饭相较平常更为豪华和讲究。饭后，全家人坐在一起聊聊天，看看电视。

在中国，最传统和最受欢迎的春节吃食是饺子。饺子的外形就像半个月亮，常见的是蔬菜猪肉馅。"饺子"的名字也是有寓意的。"饺"与"交"谐音，有相聚之意，而"子"为子时（半夜23点至凌晨1点）。所以在中国的传统习俗中，到了子时，家家户户都开始吃饺子，寓意团圆及辞旧迎新。

春节也是孩子们最快乐的时光，因为他们可以收到长辈送的红包。在春节期间，不能说任何不吉利的话语，因为人们会不高兴。

在除夕夜，人们通常在家观看中央电视台的春节联欢晚会。与此同时，会发大量祝福信息给亲朋好友。长辈们会给小辈们发红包，后者会报以很多祝福的话语，比如：

新年大吉！

恭喜发财！

愿您健康长寿！

放烟花曾经是春节期间最典型的习俗。人们认为噼啪作响的声音可以驱除邪灵。然而，由于后来政府考虑到安全、噪声和污染等因素，这样的活动在大城市就被完全或部分禁止了。

实际上，春节通常指一段时间，即从除夕到正月十五。过去，新年第一天，大家就开始给亲朋好友拜年。现在，越来越多的人都用电话、短信、微信来拜年。拜年可以从正月初一一直拜到十五。

正月十五是春节的最后一天，也是元宵节。这一天，人们会上街看灯，孩子们点亮自己的小灯笼来玩。最大最漂亮的灯笼是龙灯，看起来就像一条飞龙，由几个年轻人手持。

元宵节的传统食物是元宵。元宵是包有花生馅、芝麻馅、果酱馅等各种馅料的糯米小圆球，一般认为其形状就像天上的满月，代表团圆。这种甜点特别受孩子们的欢迎。

元宵节的传统活动是猜灯谜。通常在元宵节晚上，人们在大街小巷都会看到写有谜语的灯笼，猜出谜底的人可以获得小奖品，他们也会为自己的聪明才智而感到高兴和自豪。

过了这一天，一般人家就觉得年过完了，应该安心工作了。

Exercises

Ⅰ *Answer the questions after reading Text A.*

1. What is your understanding of the Spring Travel?

2. Why is it said that "only those who have been on the long-distance trains, and have gone through the Spring Travel, can really understand China, and can be thought as a real Chinese"?

Ⅱ *Match the Chinese expressions in Column A with the English expressions in Column B.*

Column A	Column B
1. 福	couplets
2. 春联	red packet/red envelope
3. 团圆饭	"*Fu*" Character
4. 饭店年夜饭	Reunion Dinner
5. 中央电视台春节联欢晚会	best wishes for the year to come!
6. 祝福短信	blessing messages
7. 红包	restaurant Reunion Dinner
8. 新年大吉！	CCTV New Year's Gala Evening
9. 恭喜发财！	I wish you longevity and health!
10. 愿您健康长寿！	May you come into a good fortune!

Ⅲ *Match the festivals in Column A with the Chinese expressions and dates in Column B.*

Column A	Column B
1. New Year's Day	除夕（农历十二月二十九或三十）
2. Spring Festival; Chinese New Year's Day	元旦（1月1日）
3. Lantern Festival	中国青年节（5月4日）
4. Chinese Communist Party's Birthday	国际劳动妇女节（3月8日）
5. Mid-autumn Festival	植树节（3月12日）
6. Ching Ming Festival; Tomb-sweeping Festival	重阳节（农历九月初九）
7. International Labor Day	建军节（8月1日）
8. Chinese Youth Day	国际劳动节（5月1日）
9. Dragon Boat Festival	春节（农历正月初一）

10. International Children's Day	国际儿童节(6月1日)
11. International Working Women's Day	中国共产党成立纪念日(7月1日)
12. Army's Day	元宵节(农历正月十五)
13. Arbor Day; Tree Planting Day	中秋节(农历八月十五)
14. Teachers' Day	教师节(9月10日)
15. Double-ninth Day	清明节(4月5日或4日)
16. National Day	端午节(农历五月初五)
17. New Year's Eve	国庆节(10月1日)

Micro-video

Mid-autumn Day

◎ *Text B*

Dragon Boat Festival

The Dragon Boat Festival, is celebrated on the fifth day of the fifth month according to the Chinese calendar. It was originally a festival for the ancient Chinese people to sacrifice to their dragon ancestors in the form of dragon boat races. As Qu Yuan, a poet of the State of Chu in the Warring States period (475 BC–221 BC), happened to drown himself in the Miluo River on this festival, the day of his suicide later became the festival for people to commemorate him.

The festival is best known for its dragon boat races, especially in the southern provinces where there are many rivers and lakes. A typical dragon boat is about 15.5 m in length, with a beam of about 1.1 m, accommodating two paddlers seated side by side. A wooden dragon head is attached to the bow, and a dragon tail to the stern. A banner hoisted on a pole is also fastened at the stern and the hull is decorated with red, green, and blue scales edged in gold. In the center of the boat there is a canopied shrine behind which the drummers, gong beaters, and cymbal players are seated to set

the tempo for the paddlers. There are also men positioned at the bow to set off firecrackers and toss rice into the water. All of the noise and pageantry creates an atmosphere of gaiety and excitement for the participants and spectators alike. The races are held among different villages and organizations, and the winners are awarded medals, banners, jugs of wine, and festive meals. Dragon boat races not only inherit traditional Chinese culture, but also contain the sportsmanship of solidarity, striving, and enterprising spirit. In Zigui, Hubei Province, the hometown of Qu Yuan, the dragon boat races symbolize bringing back Qu Yuan's soul to home.

Micro-video

Dragon Boat Festival

Eating *zongzi* is also a traditional custom of the Dragon Boat Festival. According to the legend, the custom of eating *zongzi*, glutinous rice stuffed with different fillings and wrapped in a style of pyramid by reed or bamboo leaves, is also to commemorate the poet Qu Yuan. Therefore, both dragon boat races and eating *zongzi* are traditional customs of the Dragon Boat Festival.

Qu Yuan was a minister of the State of Chu situated in present-day Hunan and Hubei provinces during the Warring States Period. He was upright, loyal, and highly esteemed for his wise counsel that brought peace and prosperity to the state. However, when a dishonest and corrupt prince vilified Qu Yuan, he was disgraced and dismissed from office. Realizing that the state was in the hands of evil and corrupt officials, Qu Yuan grabbed a large stone and leapt into the Miluo River on the fifth day of the fifth month. Nearby fishermen rushed over to try and save him but were unable to even recover his body. The state declined thereafter and was eventually conquered by the State of Qin.

The people of Chu who mourned the death of Qu Yuan threw rice into the river to feed his ghost every year on the fifth day of the fifth lunar month. But one year, the spirit of Qu Yuan appeared and told the mourners that a huge reptile in the river had stolen the rice. The spirit then advised them to wrap the rice in silk and bind it with five different-colored threads before tossing it into the river, which is the origin of *zongzi*.

During the Dragon Boat Festival, this glutinous rice pudding called *zongzi* is eaten to symbolize the rice offerings to Qu Yuan. Ingredients such as beans, lotus seeds, chestnuts, lard, and the golden yolk of a salted duck egg are often added to the glutinous rice. The rice pudding is then wrapped in bamboo leaves, bound with a kind of raffia, and boiled in salt water for hours.

Now Jiaxing *zongzi* is very popular in China, which can be bought all year round.

端午节

中国农历五月初五那天是端午节。最初是上古先民以龙舟竞渡的形式祭祀龙祖的节日。后因战国时期(公元前475—前221)的楚国诗人屈原在端午节抱石投汨罗江自尽,亦将端午节作为纪念屈原的节日。

这个节日最为知名的是赛龙舟,尤其是在水系发达的南方省份。一艘典型的龙舟长约15.5米,宽约1.1米,宽度可以容纳两名桨手并排坐在一起。船首有木制龙头,船尾有龙尾。旗杆上悬挂的旗帜也被固定在船尾,船体被饰以红色、绿色和蓝色的金边鳞片。在船的中央是一个有顶篷的神龛,后面坐着鼓手、击锣手和铙钹手,为桨手设定节奏。还有人站在船头放鞭炮,并把米扔进水里。这一切嘈杂声和盛大的场面都给龙舟赛手与观众带来了欢乐和兴奋的气氛。比赛在不同的村庄和组织之间进行,获胜者将获得奖牌、横幅、酒和节日大餐。赛龙舟不仅仅传承了中国传统文化,还蕴含着团结、拼搏、进取的体育精神和理念。在屈原的家乡,湖北秭归,龙舟竞渡象征着将屈原的英魂迎归故里。

吃粽子也是端午节的传统习俗。据传说,吃粽子的习俗也是为了纪念诗人屈原而流传下来的。粽子是用芦苇叶或箬叶把糯米及馅料包裹成金字塔形状的食物。因此,赛龙舟和吃粽子都是端午节的传统习俗。

屈原是战国时期楚国(今湖南、湖北省)的大臣。他是一个正直、忠诚、受人尊敬的人,为楚国带来了和平与繁荣。然而,一个奸佞腐败的亲王诬陷屈原,导致他被贬黜了。屈原意识到楚国陷入了邪恶势力和贪官的手中,于是,在五月初五那天抱着一块石头跳进了汨罗江。附近的渔民冲去救他,但连他的尸体也找不到。后来,楚国衰落,最终被秦国战胜。

楚国人民为悼念屈原,每年农历五月初五那天都要把米扔进河里喂他的灵魂。但是有一年,屈原的灵魂出现了,他告诉悼念者,河里有一只巨大的爬行动物把米偷走了。然后,屈原的灵魂建议他们用丝绸包米,再用五种不同颜色的线捆好,最后把它扔进河里。这就是粽子的起源。

为了纪念屈原,人们在端午节包“粽子”。除了糯米,通常还会加豆子、莲子、栗子、猪油和咸鸭蛋的金蛋黄等,用竹叶包裹,用禾草捆绑,在盐水中煮上好几个小时。

现在嘉兴粽子在中国非常有名,一年四季都可以买到。

Exercises

Fill in the following blanks.

Festivals	Dates (Lunar Calendar)	Origins	Significance	Major Celebrations
Dragon Boat Festival				
Mid-Autumn Festival				

Chinese Eyes on the World

Valentine's Day

Micro-video

Valentine's Day

Actually, the Qixi Festival, the Chinese Valentine's Day, is celebrated on the seventh day of the seventh lunar month. It commemorates a day on which a legendary cowherd and a weaving maid are allowed to come together after a whole year's separation. According to the legend, the Cowherd star and the Weaving Maid star are normally separated by the Milky Way (silvery river) but are allowed to meet by crossing it on the seventh day of the lunar seventh month. Even though in recent years, celebrating Chinese Valentine's Day has also become fashionable among some young people, it still seems that the Western Valentine's Day prevails over Qixi among Chinese younger generations.

The Western Valentine's Day, also called Saint Valentine's Day or the Feast of Saint Valentine, is an annual holiday celebrated on February 14. Each year on February 14, many young Chinese exchange cards, candy, flowers, or other gifts with their valentines. These customs of the Valentine's Day spread not only to China, but also to other countries.

The Valentine's Day originated as a Western Christian feast day honoring one or two early saints named Valentinus. Martyrdom stories associated with various Valentines connected to February 14 are presented in martyrologies, including a written account of Saint Valentine of Rome imprisonment for performing weddings for soldiers who were forbidden to marry, and for ministering to Christians persecuted under the Roman Empire. According to the legend, during Saint Valentine's imprisonment, the warden's daughter, a beautiful and gentle girl, fell in love with him for his dignity. But not every Jack has his Jill. Valentine was sentenced to death, because he refused to submit to the Roman government. Before the execution, he wrote a long letter to his lover, expressing his undying love for her, and not giving up his faith for the sake of love, and then he went to the execution, in a dignified manner. The day happened to be February 14. In order to commemorate this memorable day and to express the wish that all lovers will finally get married, the majority of Christians and young men and women set February 14 as the Valentine's Day.

The Valentine's Day is recognized as a significant cultural, religious, and commercial celebration of romance and romantic love in many regions around the world, although it is not a public holiday in any country. The customs of the Valentine's Day developed in early modern England and spread throughout the English-speaking world in the 19th century.

In the United States, about 190 million Valentine's Day cards are sent each year, not including hundreds of millions of cards school children exchanged. The Valentine's Day is a major source of economic activity, with total expenditures in 2017 topping $18.2 billion, or over $136 per person.

Cultural Exchange

Ⅰ *Match the festivals in Column A with the Chinese expressions in Column B and the dates in Column C.*

Column A	Column B	Column C
Chinese Valentine's Day	元宵节	农历八月十五
Lantern Festival	中秋节	4月5日
Shangsi Festival	上巳节	农历九月九日
Mid-autumn Festival	七夕节	农历七月十五
New Year's Eve	除夕	农历十月十五
Tomb-sweeping Day	清明节	农历正月十五
the WaterGod Festival	冬至	农历正月初一
Dragon Head-raising Day	春节	冬至后的105或106天
Hungry Ghost Festival	中元节	农历二月初二
Spring Festival	龙抬头	农历十二月三十日
Double-ninth Day	重阳节	农历三月初三
Dragon Boat Festival	寒食节	农历七月初七
Winter Solstice	下元节	农历五月初五

Coldfood Festival	端午节	12月21日至23日

Ⅱ *Discuss the following questions with your peers.*

1. Which festival is the biggest in your country?
2. What are some of the activities that people do on this festival?

Ⅲ *Choose one of the celebration categories below and think of a holiday you celebrate in your country that belongs to that category and describe how you celebrate it.*

New Year Spring Harvest Winter Historic Religious

Audio Material

An Ancient Poem on Mid-autumn Day

Ⅳ *Read the following poem and tell out:*

1. Which festival is the poem about?
2. What emotion can you feel in the poet from the poem?
3. Which lines in the poem do you like best? Why?

How rare the moon, so round and clear!
With cup in hand, I ask of the blue sky,
"I do not know in the celestial sphere,
What name this festive night goes by?"
I want to fly home, riding the air,
But fear the ethereal cold up there,
The jade and crystal mansions are so high!
Dancing to my shadow,
I feel no longer the mortal tie.
She rounds the vermilion tower,
Stoops to silk-pad doors,
Shines on those who sleepless lie.
Why does she, bearing us no grudge,
Shine upon our parting, reunion deny?
But rare is perfect happiness—
The moon does wax, the moon does wane,
And so men meet and say goodbye.
I only pray our life be long,
And our souls together heavenward fly!

Chapter 2 Food

Text Reading

Micro-video

Food

◎ *Text A*

Eight Cuisines

(F: Foreigner   C: Chinese)

F: Before I came to China, I was told that Chinese food is very delicious. When I am here, I find it more delicious than what I imagined. And I can see that Chinese food stresses color, smell, and taste. Is it correct?

C: Correct. Actually in Chinese cooking we pay attention to beauty of harmony, which is the essence of Chinese cooking art. The taste of food has nothing to do with the color, but when we describe good food we call it "*meishi*," the primary element of which is color because only a good color combination can arouse people's appetite. Color is emphasized in home cooking as well. Color combination is at its best with some of the traditional household dishes, such as tomatoes with eggs or green onions with tofu.

F: I assume color combination is stressed even

more with major culinary styles since I was told there are some culinary styles in China.

C: That is true. Chinese cuisine has a number of different genres, but the most influential and typical known by the public are the "Eight Cuisines." They are: Shandong Cuisine, Guangdong Cuisine, Sichuan Cuisine, Hunan Cuisine, Jiangsu Cuisine, Zhejiang Cuisine, Fujian Cuisine, and Anhui Cuisine. There are essential factors complex including history, cooking features, geography, climate, resources, life styles, etc. that play a part in the development of a cuisine.

Micro-video

Boullli

Take Guangdong food for example. As it is hot and humid in Guangdong, people are mindful of the dryness-heat on their internal organs; Therefore Guangdong food is mild in both taste and color combination. You can't find a lot of hot and spicy food in Guangdong dishes because warm colors in the hot summer can be repulsive to people's appetite. Sichuan food is just the opposite. Sichuan is also very humid, but unlike Cantonese, Sichuan people choose to use extremely hot peppers to stimulate appetite.

F: A friend of mine once invited me to eat Sichuan food and I know it is really hot and red. By the way, Boiled Salted Duck impressed me very much, because it was so delicious. What kind of cuisine does it belong to?

C: That is Jiangsu Cuisine which is popular in the lower reach of the Yangtze River. It uses aquatic products as the main ingredients, and stresses the freshness of materials. Its carving techniques are excellent, of which the melon carving technique is especially well known. Its cooking techniques consist of stewing, braising, roasting, simmering, etc. The flavor of Jiangsu Cuisine is light, fresh, and sweet with delicate elegance. Typical courses of Jiangsu Cuisine include Boiled Salted Duck, Stewed Crab with Clear Soup, Squirrel-shaped Mandarin Fish, and Liangxi Crisp Eel, etc.

F: So many delicious dishes! I have a Chinese friend from the north, perhaps Shandong Province, and he told me there are also lots of delicious food.

C: It seems that he told you something about Shandong cuisine. Some people, especially those in Shandong, say that mild dishes are short of the rich taste while dark-colored dishes are short of savor. And Shandong cuisine combines the best of taste and savor. Shandong cuisine tends to highlight taste and color in order to satisfy the needs of both.

F: That's interesting. Can you talk more about the others of those eight culinary styles in China?

C: OK. Have you ever tried Fish Head with Chopped Chili? That is the typical dish in Hunan Cuisine. Hunan Cuisine lays a stress on the use of oil, dense color, and techniques that produce crispness, softness, and tenderness as well as the savory flavors and spices. Braised Fins in Brown Sauce, Sauté Fresh Cabbage with Chestnuts, Dong'an Chicken, and Spring Chicken, are of the highest reputation. Chairman Mao, together with other leaders, praised Hunan Cuisine in 1958, which is the pride of Hunan people.

F: Wow, I am going to try it sometime next week. Then what about dishes in Zhejiang?

C: Zhejiang Cuisine is characterized by fresh, tender, soft, smooth, sweet, glutinous, and refreshing flavor. It consists of Hangzhou, Ningbo, Shaoxing, and other local food, which is marked by Hangzhou's fineness and diversification, Ningbo's softness and originality, and Shaoxing's pastoral interests.

F: Yes, I have found that, too.

C: Then come to Fujian Cuisine. Seafood is indispensable to Fujian Cuisine. Fujian Cuisine has four distinctive features, that is, fine cutting techniques, alternative soups, unique seasonings, and exquisite cooking. Chefs can always cut the thin jellyfish into three pieces and into very thin thread. And thanks to the abundant resources of marine products, the soup of this cuisine genre has its freshness

and keeps its own savor with ease. The seasonings add sweet and sour flavors to the dishes. To add to its appeal, the food is served up in or on elegant bowls or plates.

F: It sounds good.

C: Among the dishes on the Anhui Cuisine menu, you will find less fried or quick-fried dishes than those that are braised, steamed, and stewed. People here are inclined to add ham as a seasoning and sugar candy to enrich the freshness and are quite accomplished at the art of cooking. They are experts especially in cooking delicacies from land and sea. Stewed Chicken with Bamboo Shoots Soup, for example, is a very famous dish in Anhui Cuisine.

F: It seems that appealing dishes are countless.

C: That's true. In other places there are also great tastes and no matter where you visit, there will be fascinating food that you can enjoy.

Micro-video

Jiaozi

F: By the way, I was told that a serving of fruit signals the end of a meal in China. Is it right?

C: Yes, that's right. In China, fruit is also symbolic. Oranges symbolize happiness, apples symbolize peace, pomegranates symbolize fertility, and peaches symbolize longevity.

八大菜系

（F:外国人　C:中国人）

F:我来中国之前就听说中国菜很好吃,来了以后发现比我想象的还要好吃。我觉得中国菜强调色香味俱全,对吗?

C:是的。中国烹饪注重的是色香味俱全,这是中国烹饪艺术的精髓。食物的口感本来与颜色无关,但是我们形容好吃的食物时称之为"美食",其首要元素是颜色,因为只有美的颜色组合才能激发人们的食欲。即使是在家庭烹饪中我们也强调颜色的搭配,比如一些传统的家庭菜肴中,西红柿炒鸡蛋或小葱拌豆腐,颜色都搭配得非常好。

F:我听说中国有好多大菜系,我想各大菜系更看重菜品的色泽吧。

C:对的。中国菜有很多不同的流派,但最具影响力和代表性的是八大菜系,即鲁菜、粤菜、川菜、湘菜、苏菜、浙菜、闽菜和徽菜。形成一种菜系的基本要素是复杂的,包括历史、烹饪特征、地理、气候、资源、生活方式等。

以粤菜为例。因为广东地区又热又潮,人们对去除五脏之火就特别上心,因此粤菜的口味和颜色都比较温和。粤菜鲜有辛辣的食物,因为在炎热的夏日暖色调的食物会让人没有食欲。川菜则正好相反。四川也很潮湿,但和广东人不同,四川人选择用非常辣的辣椒来开胃。

F:有个朋友带我去吃过川菜,确实是又辣又红。对了,我还吃过盐水鸭,太好吃了,让人难以忘怀。盐水鸭属于什么菜呢?

C:那属于苏菜。苏菜盛行于长江下游地区。它以水产为主要材料,强调材料的新鲜。苏菜雕工精细,尤以瓜雕见长。烹饪手法包括蒸煮、焖炖、烧烤以及慢炖等。苏菜口味清淡、鲜嫩微甜,精美雅致。苏菜的招牌菜有盐水鸭、清汤蟹肉、松鼠桂鱼、梁溪脆鳝等。

F:这么多好吃的菜哇!我还有个中国朋友来自北方,好像是山东的,他和我说他们那里也有很多很好吃的菜。

C:你说的是鲁菜。有人,尤其是有些山东人,认为清淡的菜肴缺少浓郁的味道,而色泽深的菜肴则缺乏品味。鲁菜则把两者相平衡了。鲁菜注重味道和颜色,能同时满足口味和品味两方面的需求。

F:有意思。你能再说说中国八大菜系中其他菜系的特点吗?

C:没问题。你吃过剁椒鱼头吗?这是湘菜的特色菜肴。湘菜油重色浓,注重用很多香料烹制出香辣、香鲜、软嫩的菜肴,红烧鱼鳍、栗子烧白菜、东安鸡、神仙鸡都是最具盛名的。毛主席和其他领导人曾在1958年盛赞湘菜,这一直为湖南人所骄傲。

F:哇,我打算下周去试试湘菜,那么浙菜如何呢?

C:浙菜的特点是鲜、嫩、软、滑、香、糯、清爽。它由杭州、宁波、绍兴及其他地方菜组成,其中人们普遍认为杭州菜精致而多样,宁波菜柔软、原汁原味,而绍兴菜尤以田园风情见长。

F:还真是,我也发现了。

C:再看闽菜吧。海鲜对闽菜来说是必不可少的。闽菜有四大特色:刀工精妙、汤菜考究、注重调味、烹调精细。厨师们总是可以把已经很薄的海蜇切成三片,再切成细丝。丰富的海产品使得该菜系的汤不仅新鲜,而且可以轻松地保持其自身的风味。调味料给菜肴增添了甜酸的风味。为了增加它的吸引力,福建人总是把食物盛在非常好看的碗盘里。

F:听起来不错。

C:徽菜擅长烧、炖、蒸,而炒或爆炒少。安徽人喜欢把火腿和糖作为调味料提鲜,而且在烹饪艺术上也颇有建树。徽菜向以烹饪山珍海味而著称,其中竹笋煲鸡就是道不错的菜。

F:似乎好吃的菜肴数不胜数啊。

C:是啊。除了这八大菜系外还有很多别的好吃的菜,总之,无论你去哪里,都会有你喜欢的美食。

F:顺便问一下,我听说在中国,上水果就标志着一顿饭的结束。是这样的吗?

C:是的。在中国,水果还具有象征意义:橘子象征幸福,苹果象征平安,石榴象征多子,桃子则是长寿的象征。

Exercises

Ⅰ *Please write down the typical dish or main features of each cuisine.*

Cuisine	Typical Dish or Main Features
Shandong Cuisine	
Guangdong Cuisine	
Sichuan Cuisine	
Hunan Cuisine	
Jiangsu Cuisine	
Zhejiang Cuisine	
Fujian Cuisine	
Anhui Cuisine	

Ⅱ *Match the Chinese food in Column A with the English translation in Column B.*

Column A	Column B
1. 剁椒鱼头	seafood
2. 豆腐	Stewed Chicken with Bamboo Shoots Soup
3. 海鲜	tofu
4. 竹笋炖鸡汤	Fish Head with Chopped Chili
5. 红烧鱼鳍	Spring Chicken
6. 栗子炒白菜	Braised Fins in Brown Sauce
7. 神仙鸡	Sauté Fresh Cabbage with Chestnuts

◎ Text B

Deadly Delicious

(F: Foreigner C: Chinese)

F: When I was angry yesterday, one of my Chinese friends asked me to eat more tofu and green beans, which can decrease internal heat. I was confused about what that meant.

C: Well, traditional Chinese medicine believes people need a balance of *yin* and *yang* to be healthy. For example, if you are often weak and tired, maybe it's because you have too much *yin* in your body, and you should eat hot *yang* foods, like beef. Eating *dangshen* and *huangqi* herbs are also effective. While people who are stressed out and get angry easily may have too much *yang*. Traditional Chinese medicine believes that these people should eat more *yin* foods like tofu.

F: It seems that I really have to eat more tofu.

C: One should be careful not to eat too much of either *yang* or *yin* food. How much *yang* or *yin* food one should eat depends on many elements, such as season, cooking method, cooking seasoning, the individual's constitution, etc.

F: Oh, it's a little complicated for me to understand.

C: There are more stresses on Chinese food. The Chinese ancients also took the relationships of inter-generation and inter-restriction among the five elements, namely Metal, Wood, Water, Fire, and Earth, to discuss and infer the mutual relationships and the complicated laws of movement and changes among things, including food.

F: It's not so easy for me to grasp it in a short time.

C: Have you watched the film *Deadly Delicious*? Maybe that film can make it easier to understand Chinese food.

F: Not yet. What is it about? Chinese food?

C: The movie of *Deadly Delicious* just finds its inspiration in inter-generation and inter-restriction of traditional Chinese delicacies.

F: Nothing special.

C: Jiaqiao was struck with sudden physical pains, plus his eyebrows and hair began to thin, and he began to feel weak. Consultations with doctors yield proposed remedies, but few actual cures. Finally, during an acupuncture treatment, one doctor discovered that Jiaqiao had been poisoned.

F: It uses a common theme, food and relationships, to essentially tell a horror story of humanity. Can food really do that?

C: Not exactly. Experts point out that the power of the food's inter-restriction is much exaggerated in the film.

《双食记》

（F:外国人　C:中国人）

Micro-video

Food—Yin & Yang

F:昨天,我正在生气的时候,一个中国朋友让我多吃豆腐和青豆,说是这样可以降降火。这是什么意思?

C:传统中医认为,人需要阴阳平衡来保持健康。例如,如果你时常感到虚弱和疲惫,也许你是阴气太盛,你应该吃些热性的食物,比如牛肉。吃党参和黄芪也很对症。相反,压力过大和易怒的人可能是阳气太盛,中医认为他们应该多吃凉性食物,比如豆腐。

F:看来我是要多吃豆腐了。

C:热性或凉性食物都不能吃太多,热性及凉性食物的摄入量应视时令、烹饪方式、烹饪调料及个人体质等因素而定。

F:这个对我来说有点难理解了。

C:中国食物还有更多讲究呢。中国古人还利用五行(五行是指金、木、水、火、土五种基本物质元素)的相生相克关系,来探讨和推断所有事物,包括食物之间的相互关系及复杂的运动规律和变化规律。

F:一时半会儿我还真理解不了。

C:你看过电影《双食记》吗?也许这部电影会让你更容易理解中国食物。

F:没有。是讲什么的?是讲中国食物的吗?

C:《双食记》电影的灵感就来源于中国传统美食中的相生相克说法。

F:听上去没什么特别的。

C:男主人公家桥出现了身体上的疼痛。他的眉毛和头发开始变得稀疏,而且开始感到虚弱。医生也束手无策,找不到真正有用的治疗方法。最后,在一次针灸治疗中,一名医生发现家桥是中毒了。

F:看来这部电影用了一个常见的主题——食物和人际关系——来讲述一个人类恐怖故事。食物真的能做到这样吗?

C:也不尽然。专家指出,影片中食物之间相克作用的力量被过分夸大了。

Exercises

Ⅰ *Answer the following question after reading the text.*

What is your idea about *Deadly Delicious*?

Ⅱ *Match the items in Column A with the items in Column B.*

Column A	Column B
1. inter-generation	滋补饮食
2. inter-restriction	药膳
3. tonic diet	相生
4. herbal cuisine	热性食物
5. *yang* food	日常生活
6. daily life	相克

Chinese Eyes on the World

Kimchi

(R: Reporter　C: Chef)

R: Hi there. I'm doing a story about Asian cuisine and wonder if you could give me some details about Korean food? I'm particularly interested in kimchi.

Micro-video

Kimchi

C: Of course! Well, kimchi is basically a salted, pickled vegetable dish, often served us a basic side dish in any Korean meal. The fermentation of different vegetables, complemented by salted fish and other seasonings, gives it a unique flavor. It's also a nutritious dish, providing vitamins, lactic acid, and minerals. Kimchi can also be preserved for a long time.

R: OK, so pickles. Is there more than one type of kimchi?

C: Yes. There are many types of kimchi. Whole cabbage kimchi is the basic one. The cabbage isn't actually whole though; it's cut in half lengthways. Next is wrapped kimchi, where seafood, fruit, and many other ingredients are wrapped inside cabbage leaves.

R: Mmmm... That one sounds lovely. It smells good too.

C: It's delicious. We can try some later. As to white cabbage kimchi, it is less watery than other types. It uses more pickled fish and red pepper, too. Then, stuffed cucumber kimchi, which can be done by using baby cucumbers. Followed by hot radish kimchi, where the white radishes are cut into small cubes.

R: OK, I see. There are so many! Are there any other?

C: Yes, over here we have whole radish kimchi, using whole small, salted radishes. Next we have radish water kimchi, which is made without red pepper powder. And finally, water kimchi is made of thinly sliced radish and cabbage, watercress, and spring onions.

R: Wow! And this is just a selection? Which is your favorite?

C: I have to say I enjoy the stuffed cucumber kimchi. It is suitable for spring and summer, when most people lose their appetite. Cucumbers are fermented after being stuffed with different seasonings. The crunchiness and fragrance of well-fermented cucumber make them a true delicacy. Only the desired amount can be prepared at one time as it easily turns sour. Which would you like to try?

R: All of them! But, I think I'll try the wrapped kimchi. That one sounds the most interesting to me.

Cultural Exchange

Ⅰ *Try to learn how to make Chinese dumplings.*

Ⅱ *Create a one-page advertisement for your favorite food.*

Describe how it tastes, looks, and makes you feel when you eat it. You can also include a drawing to show how good it looks.

Pin or tape your advertisement to the wall with your classmates' advertisements and see how many of you choose the same food.

Ⅲ *Make a survey of foods that people don't like to eat.*

Talk to five people outside the classroom. Ask them questions about each of the foods below.

Have you ever eaten...?

If so, did you like it/them? Or if not, would you be willing to eat it/them?

There are four different ways to answer the questions:

A. Yes, I'd like to eat it/them.

B. Yes, but I didn't like it/them.

C. No, but I'd be willing to eat it/them.

D. No, and I wouldn't be willing to eat it/them.

Micro-video

Sushi

Foods

dog meat	frog's leg	snake
horse meat	bear's paw	pork
snail	calf's liver	corn on the cob
raw fish	animal intestine	peanut butter
alligator	oyster	raw vegetable salad
hot dog	beef	cheese
milk	brains	monkey meat
pizza	ant	yogurt
sheep's eye	beef tongue	noodles with tomato sauce

After you finish your survey, compare your answers with your classmates'. Are their answers similar or very different?

Ⅳ *Play a game.*

Can you guess what kind of food it is just according to its ingredients?

Ingredients: rice, soy sauce, mustard, seaweed

Ⅴ *Enjoy the following idioms on food.*

Do you know the meanings of the following idioms?

fig, leaf

talk, turkey

say turkey to one and buzzard to another

have a turkey on one's back

as poor as Job's turkey

swell like a turkey

red as a turkey cock

freckled as a turkey egg

nest egg

have eggs on the spit

run with the hare and hunt with the hounds

The pumpkin has not turned into a coach.

Extended Reading

Chinese Food: Dishes, Cooking Styles, Table Manners

Chapter 3 Traditional Chinese Medicine

Text Reading

Micro-video

Gua Sha

◎ *Text A*

Traditional Chinese Medicine

(F: Foreigner C: Chinese)

F: Yesterday I watched a film named *The Gua Sha Treatment*. In the film, Grandfather Xu came from China to visit the family of his son, Datong Xu, in St. Louis. He gave his grandson, Dennis Xu, a treatment of *Gua Sha* to treat a slight fever there. Social workers, however, mistook the traditional Chinese medical treatment which was said to be harmless for child abuse due to the obvious marks left on Dennis' back. I can't understand that kind of treatment, either.

C: It is really difficult for you to understand traditional Chinese medicine.

F: It is said that modern science has found no evidence for the basic principles of traditional Chinese medicine. It had similarity with Western medicine's scientific method in the past, but much of it is based on subjective interpretation of ancient dogma.

C: To some point it is true, but traditional Chinese medicine has been used for over 2,100 years. Before Western medical therapy was introduced into China, traditional Chinese medicine had been used as the mainstream form of medical therapy for over 2,000 years and saved millions of Chinese lives. The first historical record of traditional Chinese medicine was the *Yellow Emperor's Classic of Internal Medicine* written around 150 BC.

F: It seems that traditional Chinese medicine is an indispensable part of the splendid classic Chinese culture originating in antiquity. In its long course of development, it has summarized the experience of the Chinese people in fighting against diseases.

C: Yes. Actually it is rich in theory and practical in treatment. The core belief of traditional Chinese medicine is about the *yin-yang* or *qi* balance in the body and its organs.

F: What is *qi* believed to be?

C: It is believed that *qi* is life energy, and its flow in the body depends on the environment and what happens to the body. The balance of *qi* in the parts of the body depends on the flow of various kinds of *qi* and fluids. Injury, physical suffering, and lack of proper food causes a *qi* deficiency.

Micro-video

Chinese Medicine

F: What about *yin qi* and *yang qi*?

C: Most traditional Chinese medicine practitioners think that there are many kinds of *qi*, and the most basic kinds are *yin qi* and *yang qi*. Everything is a balance of *yin* and *yang*. *Yin* is coldness, darkness, gathering things, and will become an entity. *Yang* is for heat, light, and transformation, especially the transformation of *qi*. Females have more *yin qi*, and males have more *yang qi*. It is theorized that every person and part of the body has an ideal point of a balance of *yin* and *yang* for optimal health. Some ways are more appropriate for increasing *yang qi*, and some are appropriate for decreasing *yang qi*, and likewise for *yin qi*.

F: I think I have got it. The core idea of traditional Chinese medicine is that people can increase or decrease the various *qi* in the body, and in its parts, by various medical techniques, to create a healthful *yin-yang* balance. Then how does traditional Chinese medicine balance *qi* for better health?

C: It is believed that *qi* deficiencies (i.e. poor health) in a person or a body part can be corrected by eating proper food, taking herbs and medicines, using physical manipulation such as cupping, moxibustion, acupuncture, and massage, or doing meditation and physical exercise such as *qigong*. For example, if a woman is sick or weak due to the lack of *yin qi*, she can eat food nourishing *yin qi*, such as melons and goji berries, or take various herbs nourishing *yin qi*.

F: No wonder it is a style of traditional medicine built on a foundation of more than 2,100 years of practice of Chinese medicine. By the way, I once saw a doctor of traditional Chinese medicine examine the patient's tongue and the pulse. Does it work?

C: Actually, four classical diagnostic methods are used in the diagnosis process of traditional Chinese medicine. These four methods include inspection, auscultation and olfaction, inquiry, and palpation. The examination of the tongue and the pulse are among the principal diagnostic methods in traditional Chinese medicine, namely inspection and palpation. Certain sectors of the tongue's surface are believed to correspond to the *zàng-fǔ*. For example, teeth marks on some part of the tongue might indicate a problem of the heart, while teeth marks on another part of the tongue might indicate a problem of the liver.

F: It is amazing.

C: It is surely complex. Pulse palpation involves measuring the pulse both at a superficial and at a deep level of three different locations on the radial artery of each arm, for a total of twelve meridians, all of which are thought to correspond with certain *zàng-fǔ*. The pulse is examined for several characteristics including rhythm, strength, and volume, and is described with qualities like "floating, slippery, feeble, thready, and quick"; each of these qualities indicates certain diseases.

F: Learning the pulse palpation must take several years! Traditional Chinese medicine is really amazing.

中 医

(F:外国人　C:中国人)

F:昨天我看了一部电影叫《刮痧》。在这部电影中,许大爷从中国到圣路易斯看望儿子许大同一家。在那里,他用刮痧疗法给孙子丹尼斯治疗轻微低烧,据说这是无害的中医治疗方法。然而，那里的社会工作者误以为他是在虐待儿童，因为丹尼斯的背上留下了明显的痕迹。我也不理解这种疗法。

C：对于你们来说要理解中医确实不容易。

F：据说现代科学没有发现支持中医基本原理的证据。中医与西医的科学方法过去曾有相似之处，但中医大部分是基于对古训的主观解释。

C：从某种程度上说这是真的。但是中医的应用已有2100多年的历史了。在西医疗法传入中国之前，中医已经被作为主流医学疗法使用了2000多年，挽救了千千万万中国人的生命。最早的中医历史记载是公元前150年左右的《黄帝内经》。

F：看来中医是古代中国灿烂的经典文化中不可或缺的一部分。它在漫长的发展历程中，总结了中国人民抗击疾病的经验。

C：是的。实际上它在治疗上具有丰富的理论和实践意义。中医的核心理念是阴阳或气在身体和器官上的平衡。

F：气是什么？

C：人们相信气是生命的能量，它在体内的流动取决于环境和身体的变化。气在身体各部位的平衡取决于各种气液的流动。伤痛和身体所需食物摄入不足都会导致气虚。

F：阴气和阳气呢？

C：大多数中医认为气的种类繁多，而最基本的是阴气和阳气。万事万物都是阴阳平衡的。阴为寒，为暗，为聚，为实体化；阳为热，为光，为化，为气化。女性有较多的阴气，男性有较多的阳气。从理论上讲，每个人及其身体的每一部分都有一个理想的阴阳平衡点，以达到最佳的健康状态。有些方法更适合增加阳气，有些更适合减少阳气，阴气也如此。

F：我想我明白了。中医的核心理念是，人们可以通过各种各样的医疗技术来增加或减少身体及各器官内的各种气，从而创造一个健康的阴阳平衡。那么中医如何平衡气来改善人们的健康状况呢？

C：人们认为，整个人或身体某部位的气虚（即健康状况不佳）是有好些方法可以使之得到改善的。可以通过吃某些滋补的食物、草药和其他药物，还有理疗，比如拔火罐、艾灸、针灸和按摩，或者做冥想和身体锻炼，比如气功。例如，如果一个女人因阴气不足而生病或虚弱，她就可以吃滋阴的食物，如瓜、枸杞，或吃各种滋阴的草药。

F：中医不愧是一种传统医学的风格，不愧是在2100多年的中医实践基础上建立起来的一种治病理念。对了，我曾看到一名中医检查病人的舌头和脉搏。这能看出什么吗？

C：实际上，中医在诊断过程中采用的是经典的四诊：望、闻、问、切。舌诊和脉诊是中医的主要诊断方法：望诊和切诊。舌头表面的各个区域被认为与身体脏腑对应。例如，舌头某一处的齿痕可能表明心脏有问题，而另一处的齿痕则可能表明肝脏有问题。

F：难以置信。

C：当然这是很复杂的。脉诊通过测量每只手的桡动脉寸关尺三处的表层及深层的脉象来了解身体十二经脉的情况，所有这些都被认为与某些脏腑相对应。脉诊主要是检查以下几个特征：快慢、强弱和深浅，常见病脉有浮脉、滑脉、虚脉、细脉、数脉等。

F：看来学习脉诊一定需要好几年的时间。中医真是太神奇了！

Exercises

Ⅰ *Look at the pictures and tell out the diagnostic / main treatment methods in traditional Chinese medicine.*

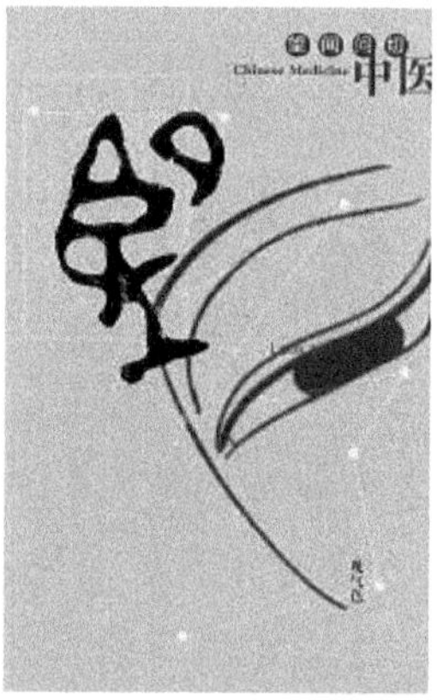

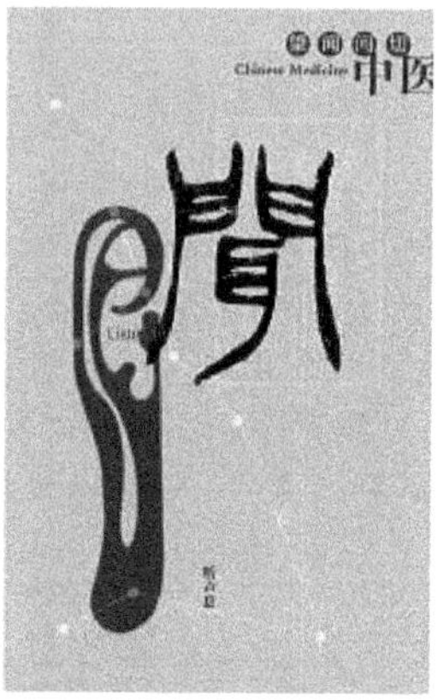

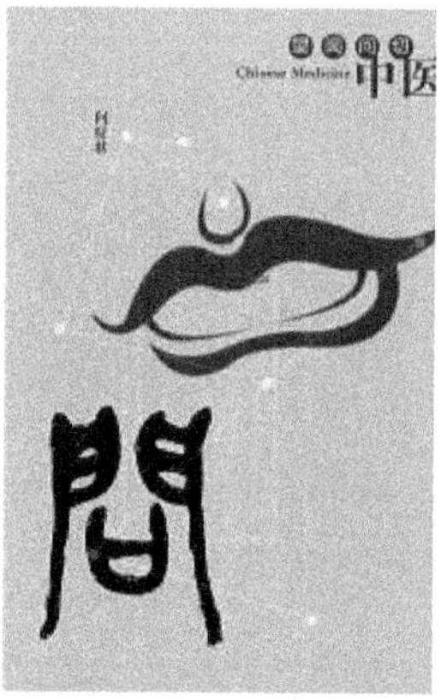

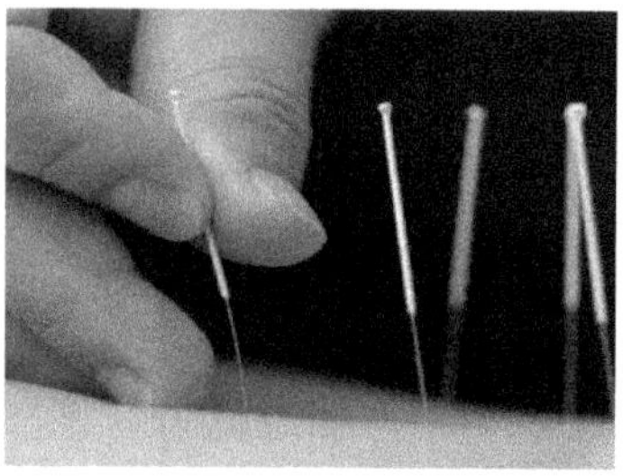
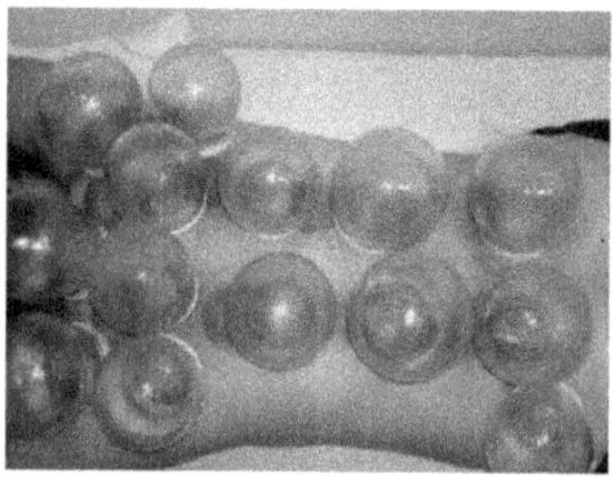
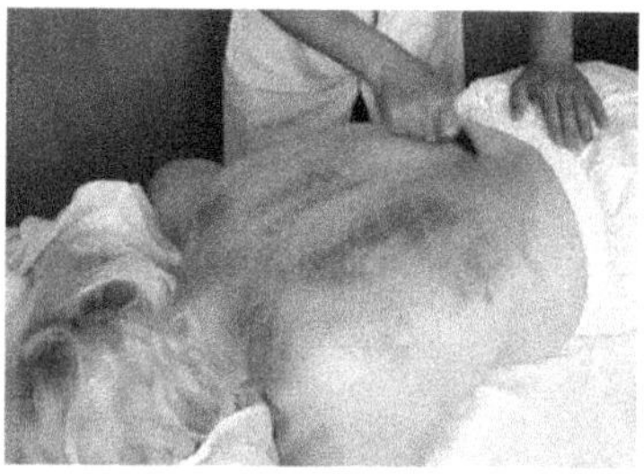

Ⅱ *Please fill in the blanks according to the law that yin and yang are two opposite aspects.*

Yin	*Yang*
abdomen	back
deep	
	hollow organs

Continued

Yin	*Yang*
solitude	
	exterior of the body
wet	
	motion
anatomy	
	warm
inward qi flow	

◎ *Text B*

Basic Vocabulary of Traditional Chinese Medicine Formulas

Traditional Chinese medicine formula is a subject dealing with the therapeutic methods and the theories of compatibility of formulas as well as the clinical application. A formula is composed of different traditional Chinese medicines and suitable doses in their rational combination.

Audio Material

Basic Vocabulary of Chinese Medical Formulas

The following are special terms in trational Chinese medical formulas.

principle	method
formula	medicine
diaphoresis	emesis
purgation	harmonizing
warming	clearing
tonifying	dispersion
sovereign medicine	minister medicine
assistant medicine	envoy medicine
modification of a formula	preparation
decoction	powder
pill: honeyed pill, watered pill, flour and water paste pill, concentrated pill, dripping pill	paste: decocted extract, ointment, plaster
wine	pellet
medicinal tea	distillate
lozenge	stripe
thread	suppository
granules	tablet
syrup	capsule
oral liquid	injection
moxibustion formula	aerosol
enema	compression formula
liniment	superficies-relieving formula
purgative formula	harmonizing method
heat-clearing formula	heat-clearing formula
warming interior formula	wind-relieving formula
dryness-relieving formula	desiccating formula
phlegm-expelling formula	digestive formula
anti-helminthic formula	emetic formula
tonifying formula	astringent formula
sedative	formula for resuscitation
carminative formula	blood-regulating formula

The advantages of traditional Chinese medicine formulas can be illustrated in the following three aspects:

(1) Traditional Chinese medicines of similar action, if used simultaneously, can strengthen the therapeutic effect for serious diseases.

(2) Traditional Chinese medicines of different actions in combination can broaden the therapeutic scope in the treatment of complex conditions.

(3) Some drastic or toxic traditional Chinese medicines may be applied with some others capable of reducing or removing their side effect or toxicity.

方剂学基本知识

方剂学是研究治疗方法和方剂配伍理论及临床应用的一门学科。一个配方是由不同的中药和适当的剂量组成的合理组合。

方剂学里的专门用语如下。

理	法
方	药
汗	吐
下	和
温	清
补	消
君药	臣药
佐药	使药
方剂加减	剂型
汤剂	散剂
丸剂:蜜丸、水丸、糊丸、浓缩丸、滴丸	膏剂:煎膏、软膏、硬膏
酒剂	丹剂
茶剂	露剂
锭剂	条剂
线剂	栓剂
冲剂(颗粒剂)	片剂
糖浆剂	胶囊剂

续 表

口服液	注射液
灸剂	气雾剂
灌肠剂	熨剂
搽剂(擦剂)	解表剂
泄剂	和解剂
清热剂	清暑剂
温里剂	祛风剂
治燥剂	祛湿剂
祛痰剂	消食剂
驱虫剂	涌吐剂
补益剂	固涩剂
安神剂	开窍剂
理气剂	理血剂

方剂的优点可以体现在以下三个方面：

(1)具有类似效用的中药,如果同时使用,可以加强对严重疾病的治疗效果。

(2)不同效用的中药联合用药可以拓宽复杂病症的治疗范围。

(3)有些含剧毒的中药可与其他中药一起使用,以减少或消除其副作用或毒性。

Chinese Eyes on the World

Differences Between Traditional Chinese Medicine and Western Medicine

Four Chinese (A, B, C, and D) are talking about the differences between traditional Chinese medicine and Western medicine.

Extended Reading

Three National Key Disciplines (Developing)

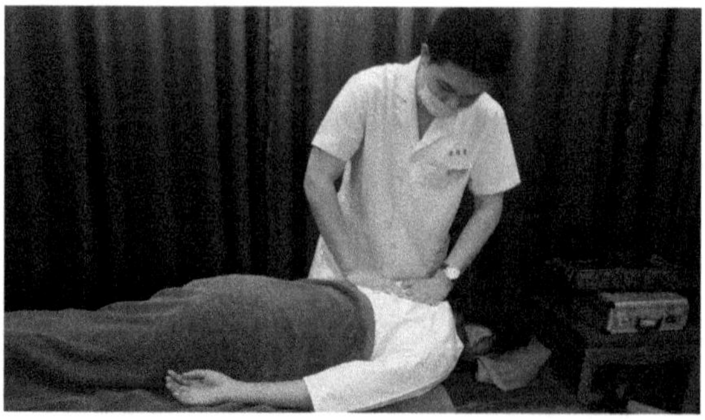

A: Many people don't know the differences between traditional Chinese medicine and Western medicine. Today, let's just talk about them.

B: The differences between traditional Chinese medicine and Western medicine are thought as a matter of perception. For any given patient with the same signs and symptoms, you will get varied ways of how the information pertaining to that patient is organized, while using either traditional Chinese medicine or Western medicine.

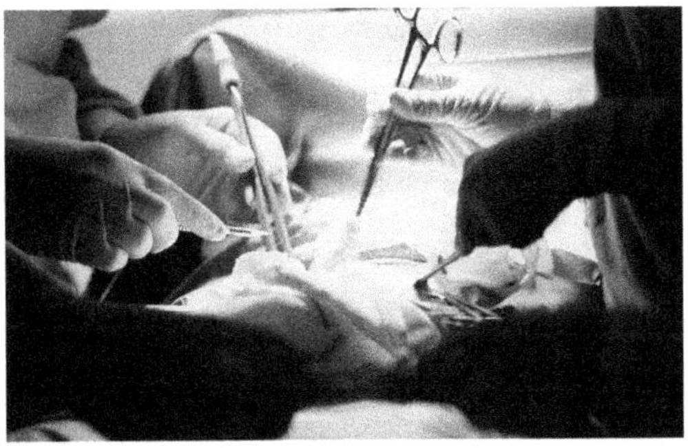

C: Yes. One major difference between traditional Chinese medicine and Western medicine is that traditional Chinese medicine prefers to treat the body as a thing, while Western medicine focuses on the main problem. The differences go deeper still and cover the philosophy of medicine, preventative action, diagnosis, and treatment. Neither one is perfeatly right nor perfeatly wrong—instead they are complementary to each other.

D: Although it is debatable whether traditional Chinese medicine is scientifically sound, you cannot deny it has a rich philosophic significance. This is very different from Western medicine. Usually, a practitioner of traditional Chinese medicine emphasizes entirety and dialectical implications. This is why some people view it as a comprehensive medicine. In contrast, a doctor of Western medicine deals with symptoms. For instance, if someone has a sore throat, a doctor of Western medicine may treat it as a throat problem while a doctor of traditional Chinese medicine may link it to the disorder of the patient's stomach.

C: One of the key differences is the approach. The approach with Western medicine is reductive and analytical, while traditional Chinese medicine uses an inductive and synthetic approach.

B: As for the downside of traditional Chinese medicine, unlike Western medicine, it lacks tools to study the detailed internal mechanisms of the human body; therefore, determining the most effective treatment in cases like infectious diseases becomes a matter of trial and error. The abundance of tools to provide powerful diagnostic functions in Western medicine makes it more precise in selecting a more effective treatment to root out an ailment. However, lately the trend is to integrate both types of medicines in treatment.

D: A doctor of traditional Chinese medicine examines his patients by using methods like inspection, auscultation and olfaction, inquiry, and palpation. His Western counterpart relies on symptoms or evidence, like body temperature and lab tests. A doctor of traditional Chinese medicine determines the problem of his patient's interior organs by observing very exterior signs such as complexion or the tongue. A doctor of Western medicine, on the other hand, makes his judgement based on the results of lab tests on the internal organs. He then reinforces his judgement by examining exterior symptoms. A doctor of Western medicine uses some chemical-based medicines and surgery, but a doctor of traditional Chinese medicine relies on herb medicines and acupuncture.

B: While Western medicine is purely a science, Chinese medicine is more of a healing art. Chemical compounds are used to formulate medications in Western medicine, but only herbs are used for traditional Chinese treatments. Almost every plant is seen to have some health benefit to the body, and as such there are perhaps little side effects of medicines, since herbs are basically administered in their natural forms. On the other hand, Western medicine relies exclusively on chemical drugs, and at the center of that medicine is a very profitable pharmaceutical industry that is responsible for the research and production of these chemical drugs. Although these compounds may have higher potency due to the extensive research done to produce them, they also come with side effects which range from mild to severe, and even fatal in some instances of drug use.

A: Maybe we can summarize it as the following:

Western medicine uses a reductive and analytical approach, while traditional Chinese medicine uses an inductive and synthetic approach.

Western medicine is standardized and evidence-based, while traditional Chinese medicine is experience-based.

Western medicine is a pure science, while traditional Chinese medicine is more of a healing art.

Traditional Chinese medicine lacks proper diagnostic tools, while Western medicine has powerful diagnostic ability.

B: In brief, Western medicine has absolute advantages in the medical fields such as the diagnosis of organic diseases, prevention of the spread of epidemic conditions, and life-sustaining activities in need of modern science and technology to support. While in the treatment of chronic inflammation, functional disorders, sub-health states, and difficult health problems, traditional Chinese medicine takes the unparalleled dominant position.

C: Yes. Traditional Chinese medicine, as an integral part of Chinese culture, has been used for prevention and treatment of diseases as well as for health maintenance and has made a significant contribution to the public health.

Cultural Exchange

Ⅰ *Discuss the following questions with your peers.*

1. Do you believe in traditional Chinese medicine? If you are ill, would you like to try it?

2. Can you try to explain the Chinese saying "Good medicine tastes bitter"?

3. When someone is sick in your country, will people have some traditional remedies instead of Western medicine? If so, can you explain it?

Ⅱ *How do you understand these English idioms? What do you think of them?*

1. Diet kills more than pills.
2. The best physicians are Dr. Diet, Dr. Quiet, and Dr. Merryman.
3. Abstinence is the best medicine.
4. Temperance and fasting cure most diseases.
5. The drunkard continually assaults his own life.

Ⅲ *Have a debate on the following topic.*

Topic: Traditional Chinese Medicine must survive into the next century or be abolished immediately.

Step 1 The class will be split into halves. One half is for the statement "Traditional Chinese medicine must survive into the next century" and the other is for the statement "Traditional Chinese medicine must be abolished immediately."

Step 2 Students in each group brainstorm for five minutes to find reasons for their argument.

Step 3 The representatives of both groups take turns presenting their respective arguments. Two or three members from each group can provide their ideas to support their representatives during the debate.

Step 4 Each representative makes a final remark based on the conclusion that his group has reached.

Chapter 4 Clothing

Text Reading

Micro-video

Chinese Mational Costumes

◎ *Text A*

Chinese Clothing Style

(F: Foreign student C: Chinese teacher)

F: Nowadays, most Chinese wear modern clothes in their daily lives, and they look not much different from the westerners. However, some differences are often seen in Chinese movies and TV dramas. Can you tell me something about Chinese clothing?

C: As a vital part of Chinese civilization, traditional clothing plays an important role in the country's history and culture. The basic features of clothing popular in China for many years in the early days were known as *jiaoling youren*, or wrapping the left lapel over the right, tying with sash and a form of blouse plus skirt or long gown. Then 1912 – 1949, Chinese Tunic Suit (Zhongshan Zhuang) and cheongsam became popular. Traditional attires are only worn during certain festivals, ceremonies, or religious occasions. And they are also often seen in Chinese movies and TV dramas.

F: Is this one in the picture "Zhongshan Zhuang"?

C: Yes. Zhongshan Zhuang is also called Yat-sen Suit. It is designed by Dr. Sun Yat-sen who combined the Western-style suit and the Chinese attire. It has a turn-down collar and four pockets with flaps. As Chairman Mao Zedong worn it quite frequently, it is also called the Mao Suit by westerners. It is the main attire for Chinese males from the founding of the People's Republic of China in 1949 till the 1980s. Today, there are still some people in China, including leaders, celebrities, and ordinary people, choose to wear Mao Suit on some important occassions, while the modern Mao Suit has been much improved.

F: Then can you show me a picture of cheongsam?

C: OK. Here you are.

F: Wow! It is beautiful.

C: As for Chinese women, when attending some important ceremonies or international events, some of them will choose to wear cheongsam. It is converted from the Manchu ethic group's costume in the Qing Dynasty and becomes a fashion in Shanghai in the 1920s.

F: Oh, look at this. Many of my friends love the dress she wore.

C: Yes. Some Chinese elements in the dress, for example, Mandarin collars, cheongsam variations, fabrics with typical Chinese motifs such as the Chinese dragon have been widely adopted by the fashion designers from both at home and abroad. Chinese elements such as clouds, Chinese dragons, fans, and bright colors are used on sports clothes and sneakers of some international brands. For example, the Nike Air Jordan China edition with dragon-inspired patterns and indigenous red silk, was the first Air Jordan shoes designed with Chinese characteristics.

F: Yesterday I saw a film about the emperor of China and his imperial robe was impressive to me.

C: Stringent rules were made for the color of ancient Chinese dress and personal adornment. Yellow was the most noble color as a symbol of power. Green, yellow, red, white, and black were pure colors exclusively for royalty and aristocracy. The common people could only apply the secondary colors.

F: Oh, I see.

C: The red color is considered as a sign of good luck. It is said to be a strong color that can keep away evil spirits. And we use red in many festive events, such as weddings.

Darker colors are favored over lighter ones in traditional Chinese clothing, so the main color of ceremonial clothing tends to be dark while light-colored clothing is worn more frequently by the common people for everyday life.

F: What I have found is that clothing varies by regions, ethnic backgrounds, and economic conditions. Contemporary urban clothing seems to have developed an obsession with brand names. In major urban centers, especially Shanghai, an increased Western look is preferred.

Chinese teenagers prefer sports brands like Nike, Reebok, and Li Ning. Younger children usually wear clothes with a cartoon character.

C: Yes. That is true. But China is home to 56 ethnic groups, whose own characteristics and traditions are expressed in their unique clothes and ornaments with distinctive decoration. Ethnic costumes are often considered to provide a record of history and folklore and to bear the totems of the national beliefs. The features of Chinese ethnic costumes are easily observed from the embroidered shoes, waistbands, silver bracelets, necklaces and earrings, and other ornaments.

中国的服装

（F:留学生　C:中国老师）

F:如今,大多数中国人在日常生活中都穿现代服装,与西方人相差不大。然而在中国的影视剧里我总看到一些不一样的穿着,你能不能给我介绍一下中国的服装?

Extended Reading

Traditional Chinese Clothing: History, Types, Features

C:传统服饰是中华文明的重要组成部分,在中国的历史和文化中占有重要地位。中国早期流行服饰的基本特征是“交领右衽”,即以左侧的衣襟压住右侧的衣襟。用腰带和衬衫搭配,再加上裙子或长裙。1912—1949年,开始流行中山装和旗袍。当然,传统服饰只在某些节日、庆典或宗教场合穿,也经常出现在中国的影视剧中。

F:这张图片上的是中山装吗?

C:是的。中山装是孙中山先生设计的西装和中式服装的混合体。它是直翻领、有袋盖的四贴袋服装。毛泽东主席也经常穿,因此它也被西方人称为“毛装”。它是1949年中华人民共和国成立至20世纪80年代期间中国男子的主要服装。即使在今天,中国依旧有一些人,包括领导、明星和普通老百姓,在一些重要场合选择穿中山装。只不过,现代的中山装进行了不少改良。

F:能给我看张旗袍的图片吗?

C:好啊。这张。

F:哇,好漂亮。

C:很多中国女性在参加一些重要的仪式或国际活动时,会选择穿旗袍。它从清代满族人的民族服饰转变为20世纪20年代上海的一种风尚。

F:哦,看这张,她这条裙子我的很多朋友都喜欢。

C:是的。现在有好些中国元素,如中式领、改良旗袍,带有像龙这样典型的中国图案的面料,已被国内外时尚设计师广泛采用。中国元素,如云、龙、扇和鲜艳的色彩,被用于一些国际品牌的运动服装和运动鞋的设计中。例如,耐克的飞人乔丹鞋中国版,运用了以龙为灵感的图案和地道的红色丝绸,是第一款具有中国特色的飞人乔丹鞋。

F:对了,昨天我看了一部关于中国皇帝的电影,他穿的龙袍给我留下了很深刻的印象。

C:颜色在中国古代服饰中有严格的规定。黄色是最尊贵的颜色,是权力核心的象征。青、黄、赤、白、黑等正色是专供皇室贵族使用的。平民百姓只能使用间色。

F:哦,这样啊。

C:红色被认为是吉祥的象征。据传它是一种能驱除邪灵的强烈颜色。人们在很多喜庆的场合,比如婚礼上,都会选用红色。在中国传统服装中,深色衣服比浅色衣服更受欢迎。因此重要场合的礼服的主色调往往是深色的,而浅色衣服则更常被普通百姓在日常生活中所穿。

F:我发现区域、民族背景、经济条件不同,着装也有差异。当代城市服装似乎很追捧品牌。在中国的大城市,尤其是上海,人们更喜欢西方风格。

中国青少年喜欢耐克、锐步和李宁等运动品牌。小朋友通常穿有卡通人物的衣服。

C:是的,没错。不过,中国有56个民族,每个民族的特色和传统都以独特的服饰来表达。民族服饰通常被认为述说了历史和民间传说,是承载民族信仰的图腾。中国民族服饰的特点很容易从绣花鞋、腰带、银手镯、项链、耳环等配饰中看到。

Exercises

Ⅰ *Fill in the blanks with what you have read in the text.*

1. Chinese traditional clothing for men is ______, and for women ______.

2. ______ is the most valuable color as a symbol of center.

3. Chinese people wear dress in ______ in many festive occasions, such as weddings.

4. China is home to ______ ethnic groups and whose own characteristics and traditions are

expressed in their unique clothes and ornaments with distinctive decorations.

Ⅱ *Answer the following question after reading the text.*

Can you see some Chinese elements in this dress?

◎ *Text B*

Well-Known Fashion: Cheongsam

Micro-video

Cheongsam

Although the fashion trend changes over time, there are several types of clothes that are popular till today both at home and abroad, one of which is cheongsam.

Cheongsam is one of the most typical, traditional costumes for Chinese women. Also known as *qipao*, it is a treasure in the colorful fashion world because of its particular charm.

Cheongsam originated from the Manchu female clothes, and evolved by merging with Western patterns that show off the beauty of a female body. It is featured by straight collar, strain on the waist, coiled buttons and slits on both sides of the dress. Materials used are usually silk, cotton, and linen. Cheongsam is the most popular Chinese attire in the world today.

The Qing Dynasty unified China, and unified the costume nationwide as well. At that time, women wore cheongsam. Although the 1911 Revolution toppled the rule of the Qing Dynasty, the female dress survived the political change and, with succeeding improvements, has become the traditional dress for Chinese women.

Till the 1930s, the lower hem of women's cheongsam reached the calves with embroidered flower patterns on it, while that of men's cheongsam reached the ankles and had no decorative patterns.

From the 1930s, cheongsam had almost been the uniform for women. Folk women and upper-class women all dressed themselves in cheongsam, which even became a formal suit for occasions of social intercourse or diplomatic activities. Later, cheongsam even spread to foreign countries and became the favorite of some foreign females.

After the 1940s, influenced by new fashion at home and abroad, there emerge various forms of cheongsams we see today that emphasize color decoration and that set off the beauty of the female shape.

The cheongsam can either be long or short, unlined or interlined, woolen or silk. Besides, with different materials, the cheongsam presents different styles. Cheongsams made of silk with patterns of flowerlet, plain lattices, or thin lines demonstrate charm of femininity and staidness; those made of brocade are eye-catching and magnificent and suitable for occasions of greeting guests and attending banquets.

Why do female Han people like to wear the cheongsam? The main reason is that it fits well their figure, and with simple lines it looks elegant. What's more, it is suitable for wearing in all seasons by old and young.

The movie *In the Mood for Love* is a romantic Hong Kong film written, produced, and directed by Wong Kar-wai in 2000. At the 2000 Cannes Film Festival, *In the Mood for Love* was nominated for the Palme d'Or and Tony Leung was awarded Best Actor. It is frequently listed as one of the greatest films of the 2000s and one of the major works of Asian films.

Many Chinese regard the film as a virtual cheongsam show. The array of cheongsams worn by Maggie Cheung is elegant, allusive, and sensual. It indicates the passage of time and beauty in a sad atmosphere, showing us how an intellectual female bonded to tradition lose her chances of seeking true love once and again.

Cheongsam features strong national flavor and embodies beauty of traditional Chinese costume. It not only represents Chinese female costume but also becomes a symbol of the traditional oriental costume.

著名的时装:旗袍

虽然时装流行趋势随时间流逝而不断变化,但有几种经典款式在国内外一直都很流行,其中便有旗袍。

旗袍是中国妇女最典型的传统服饰之一。它就是服装界的一朵奇葩,在多姿多彩的时尚界散发着它独特的魅力。

旗袍源于满族女性的服饰,是与西方式样相融合而形成的,展现了女性的曼妙身姿。它的特点是直领、收腰、盘扣、两侧开衩,常用丝、棉和亚麻等面料。旗袍是当今世界最流行的中式服装。

清朝统一中国的同时,也统一了全国的服饰。当时的女性穿旗袍。虽然1911年的辛亥革命推翻了清朝的统治,但女性的服饰在政治变革中仍得以延续,并在随后的多次改良中成为中国女性的传统服饰。

在20世纪30年代以前,女式旗袍的下摆一直延伸到小腿,上绣有花卉图案,而男式旗袍的下摆一直延伸到脚踝,没有装饰图案。

从20世纪30年代开始,旗袍几乎成了女性的制服。民间妇女和上流社会的妇女都穿旗袍。旗袍甚至成了社会交际或外交活动的正式着装。后来,旗袍甚至传到国外,成为一些外国女性的最爱。

20世纪40年代后,受国内外新时尚的影响,出现了各式各样的强调色彩装饰的、衬托女性美丽形体的旗袍,如今仍能看到各种花色。

旗袍可长可短,可无衬里可有衬里,可羊毛可丝线。此外,旗袍的材质不同,风格各异。花式、素色或细纹的丝制旗袍可展现女性的柔美和端庄;织锦旗袍十分醒目、华丽,适合迎接客人和参加宴会。

为什么汉族女性喜欢穿旗袍?最主要的原因是旗袍适合她们的身材,线条简洁,看起来优雅。更重要的是,它适合任何季节、任何年龄。

《花样年华》是一部香港浪漫电影,由王家卫编剧、制作和执导,在2000年的戛纳电影节上,获得金棕榈奖提名,梁朝伟获最佳男演员奖。该电影经常被列为21世纪前十年最伟大的电影之一,也是亚洲电影的主要作品之一。

而很多中国人视这部电影为一场实实在在的旗袍秀。张曼玉穿的系列旗袍优雅、含蓄、性感,淋漓尽致地表现了时间的流逝和那带有忧伤的美丽,向我们展示了被传统束缚的知识女性是如何一次又一次地失去了寻找真爱的机会。

总之,旗袍具有浓郁的民族风情,体现了中国传统服饰的美。它不仅代表了中国女性的服装,也成为东方传统服饰的象征。

Exercises

Match the items in Column A with the items in Column B.

Column A	Column B
1. cheongsam	国内外
2. elegant	丝绸
3. silk	《花样年华》
4. *In the Mood for Love*	旗袍
5. at home and abroad	收腰
6. strain on the waist	优雅

Micro-video

Foreign Clothing

Chinese Eyes on the World

Foreign Clothing

(C: Chinese student　F: Foreign student)

C: We Chinese think that American like casual wear. T-shirts, jeans, and sneakers are the most commonly seen dressing of most Americans. The oversized and super-soft sweater coat is the newest American development. Is that right?

F: Yes. Street-trend is popular in the US. This dressing style originated from African-American youth on the scene of Los Angeles, New York, Chicago, Philadelphia, the San Francisco bay area, Detroit, Atlanta, and Miami among others. Some guys like to wear oversized T-shirt and baggy pants without any belt, and thus showing most of their underwear. It's not only a fashion style but also a lifestyle as its cultural influence is concerned.

C: What do students wear, then?

F: What the students wear depends on the school. Sometimes, American high schools have school uniforms, which vary in clothing style and color. However, most high schools don't have uniforms. American teens usually wear jeans (skinny or flared), cute boots, flats, flip flops and brand names like Converse and Vans if allowed, T-shirts, V-neck shirts, zip-up hoodies, sweat shirts, and coats.

The typical stores for teenage girls would be Forever 21, Abercrombie & Fitch, Hollister, GAP, Old Navy, American Eagle, etc. You can't really go wrong with any of those stores. American Eagle is and probably will always be a really popular store for high schoolers and college students. You need to have more American dollars if you plan on shopping at Abercrombie & Fitch.

C: I know some well-known American brands including Express, DKNY, Calvin Klein, Guess, Tommy Hilfiger, Ralph Lauren, and Dolce & Gabanna. Can you tell me more about traditional clothing?

F: Actually, there were many different traditional clothing styles in North America originally. Nearly every native American tribe had its own distinctive style of clothing, and people could often tell each other's tribal identities by looking at their clothing, headdress, and ornamentation.

C: Different traditional clothing styles remind me of the news I've watched on TV. In the news, Chinese President Xi Jinping has made a striking appearance at the Great Hall of the People in Beijing, where he meets Fiji's Prime Minister, Bainimarama, who is also striking in a suit of black dress and leather sandals.

I'm also impressed by the clothes of government officials from Fiji on the balcony.

F: Yes. Fiji is an island country in the South Pacific. It was originally a British colony. Not only do women like to wear skirts, but men's daily clothes are also dresses. The dress, called Thoreau, is a very popular garment worn by Fijian men, which originated from the Fijian dress and has been worn by the Fijian people for generations. Even government officials in the upper echelons of Fiji, in formal ceremonial occasions, tend to dress in fine suits and wear "Thoreau."

C: That's interesting. What a colorful world!

Extended Reading

International Costume

Cultural Exchange

Ⅰ *Please discuss the following questions in your group.*

1. What kind of clothes do you usually wear when you go to school/work/the market/a restaurant/the movie?

2. Would you like to wear Thoreau in Fiji? Why or why not?

3. Are there any famous Chinese fashion brands in your country?

4. Can you list some foreign fashion brands which are also popular in your country?

5. Are there any traditional costume in your country? Could you please describe your traditional costume in details?

Ⅱ *Give your advice to your Chinese friend.*

A Chinese friend is going to your native country for a two-week visit next week. He or she can bring only one suitcase. In a letter, tell your friend what clothing he or she should and should not pack (maybe something special he or she should buy in your country).

Please write it down.

Ⅲ *Read the case of "Suits or casual dress?" and then discuss the questions with your peers.*

Case: Suits or casual dress?

Li Yue works for an American company that has its formal dress code. When Li Yue went to the company for registration, he wore a jeans and a T-shirt. His fellow employees were surprised at his lack of discretion. The boss Mr. White told him in the future he should wear suits. The next weekend the boss invited him to his house for dinner. Li Yue remembered how embarrassed he had been previously, and to insure that it would not happen again he wore a formal suit to the dinner. But to his surprise he found the boss wearing a pair of jeans and a T-shirt. The boss was of course a little confused about why Li Yue chose to wear a suit instead of casual clothing.

Discuss the following questions with your peers.

1. Why was everybody astonished at seeing Li Yue wear casual clothes at their company?

2. Why was the boss also astonished at finding Li Yue wearing a suit to his home?

Chapter 5 Love

Text Reading

Micro-video

Love

◎ *Text A*

On Love

Once most Chinese thought early love would affect one's study and was meaningless.

As a result, Chinese parents wouldn't let their children date others until they graduated from the university. Usually, according to Chinese custom, the boy that a girl was dating was expected to be her future husband.

Nowadays, most Chinese parents won't let their children date anyone until they graduate from high middle-school. Even though the guy a girl is dating is not definitely expected to be her definite future husband, it is still not regarded as a good thing for a girl to date with many guys even if in different periods.

Twenty or thirty years ago, most of the lovers are introduced by the matchmakers. But nowadays, most of the young people prefer getting a boyfriend or a girlfriend by themselves. On the other side, more and more young people are becoming "leftover men and women," especially in the big cities. The reason is complex. For example, staying at home after work is always regarded as one of the main reasons. But according to a survey by Sina. com, 37.5 percent of the nearly 5, 000 netizens queried consider "looking for a perfect man" the main obstacle that keeps young women single. New phrases like "leftover girls" and "leftover boys" are entering the modern lexicon, referring to women and men who are still single in their late 20s or early 30s.

Every New Year, the leftover men and women always face immense family pressure to find a suitable girlfriend or boyfriend and it seems that marriage is immediately on the family agenda after they graduate from the university. So when reaching a certain age, the young people are arranged blind date by their parents.

When two young people date outside for a dinner or just a cup of coffee, the boy is usually supposed to pay the bill.

When parents meet their children's boyfriend or girlfriend for the first time, they always ask the following questions: What are your parents' occupations? How many brothers and sisters do you have? What are your future goals? And even what his or her educational and financial backgrounds are.

Extended Reading

"Chain of Scorn" in Chinese-style Blind Date

中国的恋爱观

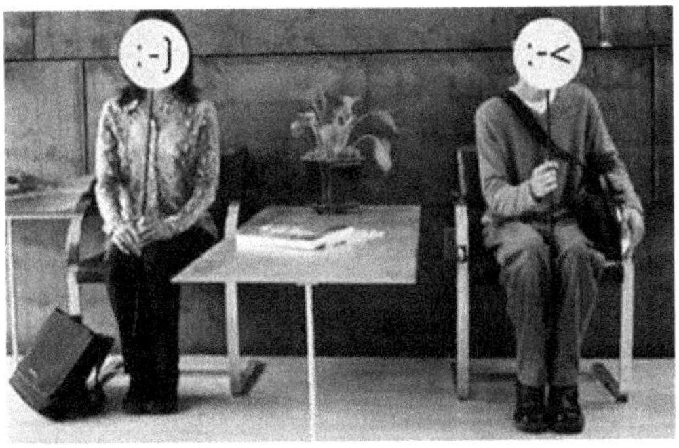

以前，大多数中国人认为早恋影响学习，毫无意义。因此，中国父母不会允许孩子们在大学毕业前谈恋爱。而且通常根据中国的习俗，一个女孩谈恋爱的对象就是她未来的丈夫。

如今，大多数中国父母在孩子们高中毕业前不会让他们谈恋爱。虽然现在一个女孩谈恋爱的对象不像以前那样一定会成为她未来的丈夫，但是人们仍然认为曾经交往过好几个男朋友不是什么好事，即使是在不同的时期结交的。

二三十年前，大多数情侣都是由媒人介绍的。如今，大多数年轻人更喜欢自己找男朋友或女朋友。但另一方面,越来越多的年轻人成为“剩男”“剩女”,尤其是在大城市。原因很复杂,例如,下班后总是宅在家里被认为是最主要的原因之一。但据新浪网曾经的一份对近5000名网民的调查,有37.5%的人认为“寻找完美男人”是使年轻女性找不到对象的主要障碍。像“剩女”和“剩男”这样的新词已经成为现代词汇,指的是近30岁或30岁出头还没有恋爱对象的单身男女。

每到新年,“剩男”和“剩女”们就会面临巨大的家庭压力:大家都在催促其寻找一个合适的对象。仿佛在他们大学毕业后,他们的婚姻问题似乎马上就被提上家庭议程。所以到了一定年龄,年轻人往往会被父母安排相亲。

当两个年轻人出去约会,不管是吃饭还是喝咖啡,通常,人们认为应该由男方来付账单。

当父母第一次见到孩子的男朋友或女朋友时,他们总是会问这样的问题:你父母的职业是什么?你有几个兄弟姐妹?你未来的目标是什么?甚至会问到其教育背景和经济状况。

Exercises

Ⅰ *Decide whether the following statements are TRUE or FALSE.*

1. Ten years ago, a Chinese girl was allowed to have a boyfriend by her parents when studying in the university.

2. Nowadays, a Chinese girl won't date more than two boys even if in different periods.

3. Most of the lovers are introduced by the matchmakers.

4. Staying at home after work is always regarded as the main reason why men and women keep single.

5. Every New Year, the leftover men and women have no family pressure to find a right person.

6. Chinese young people are seldom arranged blind date by their parents.

7. When two young people date outside for a dinner or just a cup of coffee, splitting the bill is very common.

8. When the parents meet the child's boyfriend or girlfriend for the first time, they will not ask questions about private issues.

Ⅱ *Put the following Chinese phrases into English.*

1. 约会　2. 早恋　3. 媒人　4. 剩男剩女　5. 相亲

◎ Text B

What Qualities Should a Chinese Husband Have?

Most Chinese women think that an ideal husband should have some specific qualities. Women participants in a 2018 project summed up an ideal husband's top traits with the followings.

Confidence

Confidence is the one thing that women consistently say what they want in a man. Confidence is the king, which means you will have a shot as long as you feel good about what you have to offer, and as long as you are comfortable with yourself.

Ambition

Men always think that what all women care about is money, but this is nonsense. The reason that women gravitate towards men with successful careers is because their success at work is indicative of certain attractive personality traits: commitment, discipline, and strong work ethic.

Sense of Humor

A good sense of humor is one of the qualities women always mention when listing off the things they look for in a man. A good sense of humor just means you know how to tell and take a joke.

Passion

Women love to see that you are passionate, because in their minds passion in one sphere of life can be transferred into another sphere of life.

Intelligence

Many women find that smarts is as sexy as physical appearance. Avoid running your mouth on subjects you know nothing about. Better to be suspected a fool than to open your mouth and remove all doubt.

Sociability

Women want a guy with a high social IQ. They just want to know you will not go catatonic when faced with a group of people you do not know.

Communication Skills

Sometimes, all a woman needs you to do is to lend an ear to her. It is hard for men who are always "action-oriented." If you can show a woman you have the capacity to pay attention to her, it would absolutely improve your chances.

Positivity

An optimistic person makes others feel good; his optimism can be contagious, even inspiring.

Extended Reading

7 Signs You Have a Good Girlfriend

Looks

Women are much better looking than men are. They care about men's looks too. Try to keep yourself well groomed. Wear clothes that fit, and at least make an effort to keep yourself in shape.

Independence

Women want a man who is capable and independent. He should be able to make his own decisions and can make dinner for himself. Despite what you might think, no woman wants to be your mother.

中国女人理想中的丈夫应该具备哪些特质？

大多数中国女人认为理想的丈夫应该具备一些特殊的品质。本文在2018年某项目的女性参与者的回答中，总结出理想丈夫的如下主要特征。

自信

女人一直说男人的自信是她们所喜欢的。自信就是王道，这意味着只要你对自己所给予的感觉良好，只要你对自己满意，你就有机会。

上进

男人总是以为女人只在乎钱，简直是胡说八道。女人被事业成功的男士吸引的原因是他们事业上的成功代表了他们会有一些迷人的品格：有担当、自律，以及良好的职业道德。

幽默

女人在列举喜欢的男人的品格时总会提到幽默感。拥有良好的幽默感就意味着你知道怎样开玩笑，也开得起玩笑。

热情

女人喜欢看到你充满热情，因为在她们看来，对生活中某一方面的热情可以转移到其他方面。

智慧

很多女人认为头脑和外表一样性感。对你一无所知的事情不要满嘴跑火车，被人怀疑你很笨总好过一张嘴说话就让人觉得你很笨。

善于交际

女人喜欢与智商高的男人交往，她们不喜欢你在面对一群陌生人时紧张兮兮的。

擅长沟通

有时女人只是需要你倾听，这对男人来说很难，因为男人总是以行动为主导。如果你能在女人面前表现出你注意倾听，绝对能提高你成功的概率。

积极

乐观的人会使别人感觉良好，乐观有感染力，甚至还能给人鼓励。

外表

女人比男人漂亮得多，她们也在意男人的外表。所以，你要尽量让自己的外表看上去很不错。你要穿得体的衣服，至少要努力保持好身材。

独立

女人喜欢的男人要有能力、独立、有主见，还要能自己做饭。不管你怎么想，有一点是确定的：没有女人想给你当妈。

Exercise

Match the items in Column A with the items in Column B.

Column A	Column B
1. confidence	幽默感
2. ambition	上进心
3. sense of humor	热情
4. passion	自信
5. sociability	智慧
6. communication skills	独立
7. positivity	沟通技巧
8. looks	交际能力
9. intelligence	外表
10. independence	积极

Micro-video

Love Poem

Chinese Eyes on the World

American Dating

American Dating Before 1960

In the 1920s, with dancing becoming a social activity, the young were able to spend time together without their parents, and the growth in popularity and availability of the automobile made American courtship begin to see a drastic change. Lovers had the opportunity to spend time alone with other singles on their own age, and could go on dates with multiple people before they found someone to see exclusively.

Exclusive couples often shared letter jackets and rings with the expectation that the relationship would lead to marriage.

As couples began to date younger, starting in junior high and high school, the age of marriage dropped to the late teens and early twenties, with many couples married before they began university studies. After WWII, there was a flood of marriages as servicemen returned from overseas and quickly found sweethearts, new or old, and proposed.

American Dating & Feminism

The wave of feminism in the 1960s began to change the face of American dating culture drastically. Prior to the feminist movement, women and men who did not get married could be viewed as pitiable, or possibly flawed, which prompted them to date and marry quickly.

As women began to skirt traditional roles of housewifery in favor of college, employment, and independent living, dating was prolonged and marriage was delayed.

Sexual freedom also gained prominence, with traditional dating trading for shorter, casual encounters.

Modern American Dating

Modern American dating is a product of the precedents set by the past. With many different religious traditions, personal ethics, and other guiding principles shaping different subsets of American dating, there is not one way to sum up modern dating culture. Sexual promiscuity has remained prominent, as well as problem for many girls, in particular teenagers, who find themselves pregnant and in a difficult position to support themselves and their child.

Conservative religious groups have risen partly as a backlash to these trends, stressing abstinence and prolonged courtship strictly intended for marriage. The majority of American couples have abandoned the full dating of rigor, favoring short dates over coffee or drinks over date members of their group of friends, as opposed to previous traditions of long, evening dinner dates.

High School Dance

Expanded Link

10 Best Dating Sites (2020)

Dating Website

Dating in the Digital Age

The digital age of dating has ushered in dating websites, matchmaking tools, and personality assessments to help couples find each other in an era that often lends itself to feelings of disconnect and isolation. While many people, especially women, have act ashamed of having had a date on the Internet via an online dating service, the rapid growth of dating websites demonstrates that they are in a high demand, whether or not people are willing to talk about it in public.

Digital dating allows singles to read profiles, view pictures, and compare personality traits before deciding if they would like to talk with someone or meet them. Whether or not these signs will lead to an increase in successful dates, and in subsequently marriages, remains to be studied.

Cultural Exchange

Ⅰ *Please discuss the following questions in your group.*

1. At what age do people start dating in your hometown?
2. How long should people date before they get married?
3. Is it OK to date more than one person at a time?

4. Who should pay for a date?

5. What is your idea of a perfect date?

6. What age did you have on your first date?

7. What was the worst date you have ever been on? Why was it so bad?

8. Have you ever tried online dating?

9. Which is the best way to meet someone?

10. Have you ever experienced love at first sight?

Ⅱ *Read the love poem and answer the following questions.*

1. Before reading the poem, can you tell the story of Cowherd and Weaving Girl, at a guess?

2. Which lines do you like best?

Fairy of the Magpie Bridge

by Qin Guan (1049–1100)

Thin clouds are creating works delicate;
Falling stars carry sorrows deep.
Over the vast, vast Milky Way,
Cowherd and Weaving Girl quietly meet.
Meeting in such a clear and sweet autumn night,
The rendezvous outshines many a worldly date.

Tenderness flows in the soul's retreat;
Sweet hours melt their hearts away.
The short-lived Magpie Bridge is unbearable to see,
For on the magpie-paved bridge parting comes in haste.
Ah, so long as love keeps,

Expanded Link

Fairy of Magpie Bridge

What differs, missing each other day after day!

Ⅲ *Give your relationship advice to Kate.*

Kate and Tom have been dating for two years. Kate thinks it is time to get married, but Tom has not make up his mind to get married yet.

This makes Kate think the relationship isn't going anywhere, but she loves Tom very much.

What should she do?

Chapter 6 Wedding

Extended Reading

Chinese Marriage Through a Foreigner's Eyes

Text Reading

◎ *Text A*

Chinese Wedding

(F: Foreign student　C: Chinese student)

F: In the film, I see the bride wearing a chaplet and official robes, with a red cap, and the groom wears a long red mandarin robes, which is said to be the champion robe. The palanquin the bride rode is in red, and the groom is on the horseback ride in front of the bride. That is very special.

C: Yes. That is the traditional Chinese wedding.

F: Are weddings the same in China now?

C: Not exactly. Actually, citizens in our country sometimes choose a non-religious traditional style ceremony, which quite likely related to the region or ethnic group they are from. Given the size of China and its range of ethnic groups, it is easily understood that there is much variety throughout the country. There is a growing interest in reviving traditional ceremonies.

F: I got it. Maybe not exact the same. But some elements are kept.

C: Exactly. For example, the color of red is always used in wedding as red is considered happy and auspicious in the country's culture. The most well-known wedding clothings are red cheongsam and official robes, which are still widely worn today by couples for traditional wedding ceremonies or taking wedding photos.

F: By the way, we just take photos during the wedding, how about in your country?

C: In China, most couples will choose to have professional photos and have them taken maybe as early as three or more months before the wedding. Most couples will hire costumes, perhaps the most popular is for the bride to wear a formal Western style wedding gown and the groom to wear a formal suit or a more modern stylish jackets and trousers. Alternatively, some couples choose traditional clothes. Unless you have a personal choice, the photo shoot will be at a local beauty spot and in the photographic studio so as to ensure romantic backgrounds. These photos are not only going to be put in the bride and bridegroom room, but also shown in the wedding banquet.

F: It seems that taking wedding photos is a very serious matter. But I think the wedding banquet is more important. Does it mean "reception" in English?

C: The wedding ceremony usually refers to wedding banquet in China. The word "banquet" is perhaps the best in the Chinese context, what in the English tradition is known as a "reception" or "party," where friends and relatives are entertained. Most wedding banquet will be in a restaurant and there usually holds special food, alcoholic and other drinks, too. The form of this often varies according to finances. Generally, the meal is in the Chinese way, with groups of about 10 guests around each table with a range of dishes being served over a period of an hour or so. The couple, perhaps with their immediate family, will probably move from table to table toasting the guests. China has special foods associated with weddings, again varying from region to region. There are Dragon and Phoenix cakes, meaning Happiness Cakes, something like the Western wedding cake, given to guests.

F: The couple seem to be happy and busy. Is there any other other special thing in Chinese wedding?

C: The tea ceremony which is the equivalent of an exchange of vows at a Western wedding.

F: Tea? Isn't it very common in China?

C: Here is the tea ceremony that an official ritual introduces the newlyweds to each other's family, and a way for the newlyweds to show respect and appreciation to their parents. The newlyweds kneel down in front of their parents, serving tea to both sides of parents. Parents give their words of blessing and gifts to the newlyweds. The newlyweds also serve tea to each other, raising the tea cups high to show respect.

F: That's really special.

中国婚礼

（F:留学生　C:中国学生）

F:在电影里,我看到新娘穿凤冠霞帔,还戴着红盖头。而新郎则穿着你们说的状元服。新娘坐在红色的轿子里,新郎在前方骑马。这种婚礼真特别。

Micro-video
Wedding Custom

C:是的。那是传统的中国婚礼。

F:现在中国的婚礼也还是这样吗?

C:不完全是。事实上,一些中国公民有时会选择非宗教的传统风格的婚礼仪式,这很可能与他们所在的地区或所属民族有关。由于中国地方大,民族多,全国各地的婚俗也有很多不同。不过人们对振兴传统仪式越来越感兴趣。

F:我明白了。仪式也许不完全一样,但有些元素会被保留下来。

C:没错。例如,红色总是被用在婚礼上,因为在中国文化中,红色被认为是幸福和吉祥的颜色。最著名的是红色旗袍和状元服,如今新娘新郎在传统的婚礼仪式或拍婚纱照时还会穿。

F:对了,我们是在婚礼上拍婚纱照,你们国家呢?

C:在中国,大多数夫妻会选择请专业摄影师,在婚礼前三个月甚至更早的时候拍婚纱照。大多数新人会选择租赁服装,也许最受欢迎的是新娘穿正式的西式婚礼礼服,新郎则穿正式的西装或更时髦的夹克和裤子,也有些夫妻选择传统服装。除非你有个人选择,否则照片拍摄地通常在当地风景区和摄影工作室,以确保有美丽浪漫的背景。这些照片不仅要放在新娘新郎的房间里,还要在婚宴上进行展示。

F:看来拍婚纱照是件很严肃的事。不过我认为婚宴更重要,这是否就是英语里所说的"招待宴"?

C:在中国,婚礼通常是指婚宴。在中国用"宴席"这个词再好不过了,相当于英语里的"招待宴"或"派对",就是款待亲朋好友。大多数婚宴都是在饭店里举行的,备有特别的食物，通常也有酒水饮料。婚宴的形式经常视财务状况而定。一般来说，这顿饭是中式的，每桌大约有10位客人，每桌的菜肴都会在一小时左右的时间里上齐。新人通常和直系亲属坐在一起，他们会一桌一桌地给客人敬酒。虽然不同地区习俗不同，但都会分发一些婚礼特别食品，比如龙凤蛋糕，就是喜饼，送给每位客人，有点像西方的婚礼蛋糕。

F：新人在婚礼上总是既开心又忙碌。中式婚礼还有什么特别的事吗？

C：敬茶，相当于在西式婚礼上的交换誓言环节。

F：茶？茶在中国不是很常见的吗？

C：这里的敬茶是正式的仪式，是为新婚夫妇介绍双方的家庭，以及新婚夫妇对双方父母表达尊敬和感激的方式。通常，新婚夫妇跪在他们的父母面前，为双方父母敬茶。父母给新婚夫妇送上祝福和礼物。新婚夫妇还会互相敬茶，通过抬高茶杯以示尊重。

F：真的很特别。

Exercises

Ⅰ *Decide whether the following statements are TRUE or FALSE.*

1. In a Chinese wedding the dominant tone is red.

2. Nowadays the bride usually wears a chaplet and official robes and the bridegroom wears Champion robes.

3. A Chinese wedding ceremony is very quiet.

4. Taking wedding photos is taken as a part of the wedding ceremony.

5. The wedding banquet is in the Chinese way, with groups of about 10 guests around each table with a range of dishes being served over a period of an hour or so.

6. The newlyweds kneel down in front of their parents, serving tea to both sides of parents.

Ⅱ *Match the items in Column A with the items in Column B.*

Column A	Column B
1. bride	新郎
2. groom/bridegroom	新娘
3. priest	伴娘
4. bridesmaid	单身汉
5. best man	牧师
6. bachelor	伴郎
7. married husband/wife	已婚男/女

8. wedding vows	结婚誓词
9. bridal gown	结婚礼服(婚纱)
10. veil	捧花
11. bouquet	仪式
12. ceremony	宴席
13. reception	面纱

Ⅲ *Some special terms in Chinese wedding are listed as follows.*

propose	做媒
engagement	定亲
betrothal presents	聘礼
meet the bride	迎娶
wedding ceremony	婚礼仪式
the first bow to the heaven and earth	一拜天地
the second bow to their parents	二拜高堂
bow to each other	夫妻对拜
drink wedlock wine	喝交杯酒

◎ Text B

Crying Marriage

Micro-video
Crying Marriage

Crying marriage (*kujia*), the traditional marriage custom in China in the past, was the crying and singing ceremony performed by the bride when she was married. Nowadays, crying marriage can still be found in the remote mountainous areas, especially where the minority nationalities such as Tujia, Tibetan, Yi, Zhuang, Salar, and so on live.

Crying marriage begins half a month, sometimes a month or even three months, before the wedding. But it starts off and on and the bride is free to cry. Usually when the relatives and friends come to give a gift to her, she has to cry to show courtesy. From the night before the wedding day to the day when the bride is seated in the sedan chair, *Kujia* reaches the climax. The crying in this period must be done according to the traditional etiquette. The bride who does not cry well will be ridiculed and even discriminated by

others.

The lyrics, which have been handed down from generation to generation, are improvised by the bride and her weeping sisters. The main content is to thank the parents and elders for their nurturing and the care of brothers and sisters, to sing the sorrow that the happiness of girlhood is about to pass and the confusion and uneasiness before the new life comes. In the past, there were some lyrics, such as pouring out the dissatisfaction of marriage, the hatred of the matchmaker for wrong matchmaking, and so on. Some songs of crying marriage can be said to be the crystallization of the collective wisdom of women over thousands of years, which is a unique kind of Chinese folk culture. Therefore, many people believe that crying marriage songs is a special kind of female culture, and their creation, singing, and inheritance reflect the psychology and life course of women.

Nowadays, marriage is free and the newlyweds are happy to be married, so there are fewer and fewer crying marriage. Even though there are places where you still have to cry at the wedding, it is just a ritual.

哭 嫁

哭嫁，是中国过去比较流行的传统婚姻习俗，即新娘出嫁时的哭唱仪式。现在偏远的山区，尤其是如土家族、藏族、彝族、壮族、撒拉族等少数民族所居住的地方仍有哭嫁习俗。

哭嫁一般从新娘出嫁前的半个月、一个月开始，有的甚至三个月前就已揭开了哭唱的序幕。不过，开始时都是断断续续进行的。新娘可以自由地哭。亲族乡邻前来送礼看望时，谁来新娘就哭谁，作为道谢之礼节。喜期的前一天晚上到第二天上轿时，哭嫁达到高潮。这段时间的哭唱必须按传统礼仪进行，不能乱哭。谁不会哭，就会被别人嘲笑甚至歧视。

哭嫁的歌词既有代代相传的，也有新娘和“陪哭”的姐妹即兴创作的。内容主要是感谢父母长辈的养育之恩和哥嫂弟妹们的关怀之情，泣诉少女时代欢乐生活即将逝去的悲伤和新生活来临前的迷茫与不安。过去的哭嫁也有的是倾诉对婚姻的不满，对媒人乱断终身的痛恨，等等。有些哭嫁歌可以说是千百年来女性集体智慧创作的结晶，是中华民间文化中的奇葩。所以，很多人认为哭嫁歌是一种独特的女性文化，其创作、演唱及传承，极好地折射出女性的心理及生命历程。

如今婚姻自由了，新人无比幸福，哭嫁的习俗已经越来越少了。即使有些地方依旧还有哭嫁习俗，也仅是作为一种仪式罢了。

Exercise

Answer the following questions after reading the text.

1. What does crying marriage mean?
2. Why does the bride cry in the wedding?
3. What is your idea about crying marriage?
4. Is there any kind of similar custom in your country?

Micro-video

Chinese Eye's on the World

Chinese Eyes on the World

Typical Western Wedding

(C: Chinese student F: Foreign student)

C: Western wedding seems to be a romantic type, and the whole wedding is full of an air of romance. Many Chinese girls long for a Western wedding.

F: Really? What makes you think like that?

C: Maybe at the first sight seeing a bride wear a white wedding dress and veil. By the way, I think that bride in white has a long history. Am I right?

F: Yes. A bride wearing a white wedding dress and veil was popularized by the marriage of Queen Victoria. Some say Victoria's choice of a white gown may have simply been a sign of extravagance, but many have also been influenced by the values she held which emphasized sexual purity.

C: We have seen the films depicting wedding ceremony that usually holds in a church or outdoor in a Western country, presided by a priest so that the whole wedding is regarded as the solemn seriousness.

F: Marriage in the church is the most important part of the whole wedding.

C: Can you tell us in details?

F: First along with the wedding march, the bride's father holds her hand to go in face of the groom and delivers her hands to the groom personally. The priest will ask the bride and the groom to make a lifetime commitment, which is the climax of the whole wedding. Traditional wedding vows go like the following: I, (Bride/Groom), take you (Groom/Bride), to be my (husband/wife), to have and to hold from this day forward, for better, for worse, for richer, for poorer, in sickness and in health, to love and to cherish, till death do us part.

Then the priest will give them the blessing. And the couple will exchange wedding rings and kiss each other.

C: Does the use of a wedding ring has a long history?

F: Even though it has long been a part of religious weddings in Europe and America, the origin of the tradition is unclear. One possibility is the Roman belief in the *Vena Amoris* (vein of love), which is believed to be a blood vessel that runs from the fourth finger (ring finger) directly to the heart. Thus, when a couple wore rings on this finger, their hearts were connected. Historian Vicki Howard points out that the belief in the "ancient" quality of the practice is most likely a modern invention. "Double ring" ceremonies are also a modern practice, and a groom's wedding band didn't appear in the United States until the early 20th century.

C: Nowadays, Chinese people, especially those in the cities also exchange rings in the wedding ceremony.

F: But you don't throw the bouquet according to my observation.

C: No, we don't do that.

F: The bouquet the bride holds is not some ordinary furnishing. At the end of the wedding, the bride will throw it to the female guests at the scene, which finally makes everyone laugh.

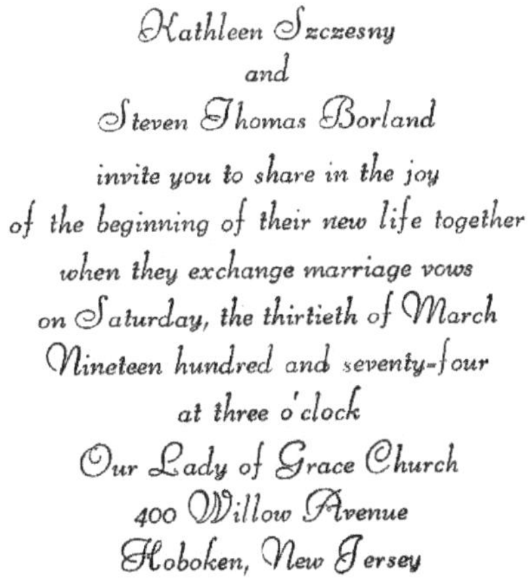

Kathleen Szczesny
and
Steven Thomas Borland
invite you to share in the joy
of the beginning of their new life together
when they exchange marriage vows
on Saturday, the thirtieth of March
Nineteen hundred and seventy-four
at three o'clock
Our Lady of Grace Church
400 Willow Avenue
Hoboken, New Jersey

C: Are there any other special activities in the wedding ceremony?

F: Taking wedding photos or videos is taken as a part of the wedding ceremony. The composition of the wedding ceremony also includes speeches from the groom, best man, father of the bride, and possibly the bride herself, the newlyweds' first dance as a couple, and the cutting of an elegant wedding cake.

C: Thank you for sharing so much with me.

Cultural Exchange

Ⅰ *Discuss the following questions with your classmates.*

1. In your culture, do the parents of either the bride or the groom give them money on the wedding day? Do they give them something else instead?

2. In your culture, when do friends and relatives give gifts to the bride and groom? What kinds of gifts are given?

3. In your culture, do married women wear a ring? If so, on which finger? Do married men wear a ring? If so, on which finger?

4. In your culture, do the newlyweds go on honeymoon together after the wedding ceremony?

5. In your culture, do the newlyweds live on their own, or do they live with either the bride's or the groom's family? If they live on their own, who is responsible for furnishing the new home usually?

6. From what you have learned or seen in movies or on TV, what do you know about American weddings? How are they similar to or different from weddings in your culture?

7. Does anything about Chinese/American wedding customs surprise you? Is there anything you like or dislike particularly?

8. When you attend in a wedding, what will you say to the newly-wed couple?

9. What kind of wedding would you like to have? Please describe your ideal wedding.

Ⅱ *Please fill in the blanks according to your knowledge.*

Cakes have played a part of weddings all through history. The 1. ______ shared a plain cake of flour, salt, and water during the wedding ceremony itself, as native Americans still do today. The traditional fruit cake originated in 2. ______, with the fruit and nuts being a symbol of fertility. It may come as a surprise to most brides that, originally, the wedding cake was not eaten by but was thrown at the 3. ______, usually by the 4. ______. And guests were encouraged to eat the crumbs that fell for 5. ______. It developed as one of the many fertility traditions surrounding a wedding. Luckily this custom evolved into actually 6. ______ the cake.

Nowadays, most people don't associate the wedding cake with having lots of 7. ______ any more. Instead, the wedding cake has become kind of a first 8. ______ for the bride and groom. Today, couples cut a slice before anyone else and feed it to 9. ______, symbolizing the support they'll provide through their relationship for many years. It is believed that an unmarried male guest who keeps a piece of wedding cake under his 10. ______ as he sleeps will increase his chances of finding a mate. An unmarried bridesmaid who does the same will dream of her future 11. ______.

Chapter 7 Family and Children

Text Reading

Extended Reading

China to Dramatically Ease One-child Policy

◎ *Text A*

Family and Children

(F: Foreigner C: Chinese)

F: Yesterday I read an English text for middle school students: "There are three in my family: my father, my mother, and me." Is that really the typical family in China?

C: Yes. In China, it is agreed that a husband, a wife, and kids count as a family. But in the countryside, more often, the grandparents are living with the young generation. And in the last 40 years or so, especially in the cities, there is usually only one kid in one family.

F: Oh, I see.

C: Due to the one-child policy over the past 40 years or so, the vast number of families have only one child. As a result, many families expect too much of the child.

F: Oh, that is not fair for the kid.

C: Yes. In the past, the relationship between children and parents in many Chinese families was not that harmonious. In a traditional Chinese family, the father should be strict, the mother should be gentle, and the children should do whatever their parents required them do and couldn't resist. Parents did all things that they thought were good for their children and didn't care about their children's feelings. While children disliked the arrangement their parents made for them, they couldn't resist directly. This, however, cannot be applied to Chinese families nowadays. There is a trend that various types of relationships develop between parents and children. But anyway, most parents are overly sheltering owing to there is only one child in the family.

F: I can understand that.

C: We have realized this problem. In one episode of "Dad, Where Are We Going?", the five-year-old daughter of former Olympic diving champion Tian Liang cried and hid behind her father when they arrived at a rural village. In an episode of another series, a young girl's face was covered with tears after being asked by her father to go out alone to buy eggs and a pancake. In the eyes of some observers, these kids show no sense of independence, and the reason is to put it down to parents who are overly sheltering.

F: Maybe these shows have led many parents to a different way they raise their children.

C: Absolutely. Liang Jing, a mother from Shanghai, said she would try to "give some training" to her shy son that she asked him to tidy up his toys. Lin Yi, a parenting expert in Beijing, said "giving kids a chance to do things for themselves helps to raise their sense of achievement, which carries benefits throughout their lives."

F: Anyway, I can see that families play an important role in children's education in modern China.

C: Yes. Chinese families are like the most ones in other countries of East Asia, in which parents value education a lot and they believe that education is the only way for kids to have a good future. So they would send their kids to various after-class training classes to learn many things besides school's classes. And it seems that they are willing to spend most of their income on education.

F: The kid is the center of a Chinese family.

C: Actually since 2016, the Chinese government

has allowed and encouraged couples to have a second child, but most young couples, especially those in cities, are reluctant to have a second child.

F: Many other countries are facing the same problem now.

中国的家庭和孩子

（F:外国人　C:中国人）

F:昨天我读了一篇中学英语课文:《我的家里有三个成员:爸爸、妈妈和我》。这是典型的中国家庭吗?

Extended Reading

The Relationship Between Parents and Children

C:是的。在中国,一个家庭一般由丈夫、妻子和孩子组成。但在农村,更多的时候是祖父母和年轻一代生活在一起。在过去的近40年里,特别是在城市,一个家庭往往只有一个孩子。

F:哦,这样啊。

C:由于中国在过去近40年里实行独生子女政策,大量的家庭只有一个孩子,因此很多家庭也把太多的期望压在孩子身上了。

F:哦,那对孩子来说不公平。

C:是的。过去很长一段时间,很多家庭的亲子关系并不是很和谐。在传统的中国家庭里,父严母慈,孩子应该对父母言听计从,不得抗拒。父母做所有他们认为对孩子有益的事情,而不关心孩子的感受。虽然孩子们不喜欢父母为他们所做的安排,但他们不能直接拒绝。当然,今天的中国家庭已经改善了许多,父母和孩子之间的关系各式各样。不过,大多数父母因为家里只有一个孩子都过于保护孩子。

F:能理解。

C:我们也已经意识到这个问题。在《爸爸去哪儿》的一期节目中,前奥运跳水冠军田亮五岁的女儿与他来到农村时,她哭着躲在父亲身后。在另一期的一集里,一个小女孩被父亲要求单独出去买鸡蛋和煎饼就哭得泪流满面。在一些观察人士看来,这些孩子没有独立意识,原因在于父母的过度保护。

F:也许这些节目让很多父母改变了他们的育儿方式。

C:当然。上海妈妈梁静说她会给她胆怯的儿子"一些训练",让他整理他的玩具。北京的一位育儿专家林毅说:"给孩子们一个机会,让他们自己的事情自己做,有助于提高他们的成就感,这对他们来说是一生受益的。"

F:不管怎样,我可以看到,在当今中国,家庭在孩子的教育中扮演着重要的角色。

C:是的。中国家庭跟东亚的大多数国家一样,为人父母者非常重视教育,他们认为教育是让孩子们拥有光明前途的唯一途径。所以他们会把孩子送到五花八门的课后培训班去学习很多课外的东西,而且他们似乎很愿意把大部分收入花在教育上。

F:在中国,孩子是家庭的中心啊。

C:实际上从2016年开始,中国政府允许和鼓励人们生二胎,但是,大多数年轻夫妻,尤其是在城市里,都不愿意生第二个孩子。

F:现在很多国家都面临着相同的问题。

Exercise

Decide whether the following statements are TRUE or FALSE.

1. A typical family in China includes father, mother, and the kid.

2. In the last 40 years or so in China, especially in the cities, actually each family has only one kid.

3. Since 2016, Chinese government has allowed and encouraged couples to have a second child, so most young couples have had a second child.

4. In the past, the relationship between children and parents in China was very harmonious.

5. Nowadays most Chinese parents do too much for their kids while they don't realize this problem.

6. In China, parents value education a lot and they believe that education is the most important way for their kids to have a good future.

7. It seems that in China parents spend much on education.

◎Text B

Who Comes First?

An American woman who was teaching in China once asked her students to put themselves in a situation where a man fell into a river with his mother, wife, and son. If the man was only able to save one person, who would that person be? Some students replied that he should save the mother to repay her parenting. Others said that he should save the son, because the child represents the future. The American teacher was very unhappy with the answers. "None of you even thought of saving the wife, why?" She asked. The students fell silent. She explained, "I think he should save

the wife first. The mother is old and has already spent most of her life. The child is too young to feel much pain. The wife has committed a lifelong partnership with him. After this incident, the couple will be bound even closer together and they can have another child."

She's definitely not talking about Chinese people. In China, a family is headed by the grandparents or parents. Children come next, followed by brothers. Marital relation comes at the bottom. On the Confucianism, a man is required to stay with his parents rather than under criticality.

There is a common phenomenon: When kids are very young, most young couples will have their parents (usually the husband's parents) living with them together. Then when the wife and the parents have conflicts, the husband usually stands in his parents' position.

Family forms the most important part of an individual's life. Any kind of tension in the family ties leads to depression and sorrow. Nowadays women's mental health is getting more and more attention. Women undergoing emotional turmoil increasingly seek advice and help from professionals to smooth things between husband and wife, which is called counseling.

关于孰先孰后的问题

一名在中国教书的美国女教师曾让她的学生假设这样的一种情况:一个男人的母亲、妻子和儿子同时掉进河里,如果这个男人只能救一个人,他会救谁?一些学生回答说,他应该救母亲,以报母亲的养育之恩。还有人说他应该救儿子,因为孩子代表未来。美国老师对这些回答很不满意。"你们谁都没想过救妻子,为什么?"她问。学生们陷入了沉默。她解释说:"我认为他应该先救妻子。母亲已经老了,已经度过了她的大部分人生。孩子还小,不会感受到那么大的痛苦。妻子已经和他结了婚,是和他相守终身的人。在这次事件之后,这对夫妇的关系将更加紧密,他们可以再生一个孩子。"

她这观点绝对不是针对中国人。在中国的家庭中,最重要的是祖父母或父母,其次是孩子,再次是兄弟,夫妻关系是排在最末位的。在儒家思想中,在危急时刻,一个男人必须保他的父母,而非妻子。

比较常见的一个现象是:当孩子很年幼的时候,大多数年轻夫妇会跟父母,通常是丈夫的父母一起生活;而当妻子和父母有矛盾时,丈夫通常会站在自己父母的立场上。

家庭是一个人一生中最重要的组成部分。紧张的家庭关系会导致抑郁和悲伤。如今,女性的心理健康越来越受到重视,并且越来越多的女性在经历情感波动的时候会主动寻求专业人士的建议和帮助，通过这种专业咨询来改善夫妻关系。

Exercise

Answer the following questions after reading the text.

1. A man fell into a river with his mother, wife, and son. If the man was only able to save one person, who would that person be in traditional Chinese situation?

What is the typical/possible answer in your country?

2. In China, when the wife and the parents have conflicts, whose position the husband usually stands in?

What about in your country?

Chinese Eyes on the World

Family Rules in America

(C: Chinese F: Foreigner)

C: Once I was told that Americans made rules for their families.

F: Yes. Family rules are positive statements about how your family wants to look after and treat the members. Rules can help everyone in your family get along better, and make the family life more peaceful. Especially, the children and teenagers learn where the rules are, and what's expected of them. The adults will be consistent in the way they treat children and teenagers.

C: Then who is to be involved in making rules?

F: It's important to involve all the family as much as possible when developing family rules. Children as young as three can help you make the rules and talk about why your family needs them.

As children get older, they can take a bigger part in deciding what the rules should be, as well as the consequences for breaking them. Pre-teens and teenagers get a lot of benefit out of being involved in making rules, because it gives them the chance to take responsibility for their own behavior.

C: That sounds reasonable. Can you tell me something more on the children educating in Western countries?

F: In Western countries, people prefer encouragement to punishment, and the punishment also offends against the law. We pay great attention to individual qualities and the emotional communication. And the happiness of each individual member does matter. While on money, we teach children to make plans for budget items and learn to spend money reasonably, and we encourage them to work in order to gain income by themselves.

C: That is a good idea.

Cultural Exchange

Ⅰ *Watch the film Juno and answer the following questions.*

1. If a high school girl is pregnant in your country, what will most parents do?

Micro-video

Parents and Children

(Review: High school girl Juno was pregnant. Now no matter how regretful Juno was, the question now is how to deal with her child in a place where abortion is prohibited in the United States. It's not a good idea to get her to work with her boyfriend Brik for life. After consulting with her confidant, Lille, she decided to give birth to the baby and then send the child out to the family who wanted to adopt the child... However, things did not go as smoothly as expected. How will Juno face the bitter fruit of this youthful impulse and ignorance?)

2. Film critic Mr. Bi Chenggong once said, "*Juno* is a movie with a big ambition of feminism as the kernel, but is interpreted lightly. By extreme kindness, devotion, and self-confidence, the feminist philosophy is upgraded as a kind of faith, which make you enjoy the story, and you can't refuse it at the same time, just being baptized unconsciously." What do you think about this?

Ⅱ *Discuss the following questions with your peers.*

1. Brian Powell is a sociology professor at Indiana University, and his team have found that "people are moving away from a traditional definition of family and they're moving towards a modern definition of family."

Do you agree on it? What is your definition of family?

2. Did you often chat with your parents (about your school life, etc.)?

3. How are children usually punished in your country?

4. Can unmarried daughters and sons move out? At what age?

5. How do parents exert influence on their children's marriage?

6. How do children express respect for parents?(By words? Obedience? Hugs and kisses?)

7. What do you think about NEET?

8. Have you been talked about sex with your parents?

Will you talk to your kids about sex before he/she goes to high school?

Ⅲ *Speak out your advice.*

One of your Chinese friends is going to your country and lives with a family for one month, thus now you are trying to tell him/her something he/she has to pay more attention to.

Ⅳ *Have a debate.*

In a group of at least four people, choose one of the parent/child issues that list below. Each group divides into two sides: One agrees with the child, while the other agrees with the parents.

Each side makes a list of reasons why their positions on the issue are correct. Then both sides present their reasons to the rest of the class. The other class members can vote to see whether they support the child or the parents.

1. A son wants to quit college for a high-paying job. His parents want him to complete his education.

2. A daughter wants to get married. Her parents do not approve of the man she wants to marry because he has no job.

3. A daughter wants to become an airline pilot. Her parents feel this is not the proper job for a woman.

4. The eldest son has been offered an excellent job out of the country. His parents do not want him to leave.

5. A child has musical talent but is only interested in rock and roll. Her/His parents object to this kind of music.

Chapter 8 Sports

Text Reading

Audio Material

Sports in China

◎ *Text A*

Sports in China

It is inevitable that with such a long history China should have developed several unique and traditional sports and pastimes. The country is so large that the various minorities are separated by vast distances. It is not surprising that they have their own special ways in which to express their vigor and enthusiasm.

Almost all the traditional sports were derived from productive activity. The Mongolians, Tibetans, and Kazakhs inhabit vast natural grasslands, and horsemanship is vital to their existence. Consequently their gifts for riding and shooting have given rise to their forms of sports. The people who live in agricultural communities or who rely on hunting for their livelihood are good at climbing, wrestling, jumping, shooting, and so on.

Micro-video

Bamboo Pole Dance

Many of these activities are accompanied by singing, dancing, and instrumental performances, which are art forms in their own right. They are mostly held as a part of the festivals like the Spring Festival and other days of significance. The Bamboo Pole Dance of the Li nationality, living in Hainan Province, is an example. The participants squat or kneel down in pairs opposite each other and hold the end of a bamboo pole in each hand. The couples bring the pole together and apart in time with the rhythm of musical accompaniment. Graceful dancers perform between the moving poles, ensuring that they maintain a rhythm that is in time with the poles so as to avoid being trapped between them. This is a very skillful and entertaining sight.

Micro-video

Pingpang Match (1)

Some sports are practiced widely by the Han nationality as well as the minority nationalities. Three most popular sports in China are table tennis, badminton, and basketball.

China has traditionally excelled in sports like table tennis and badminton at the international level. In fact, the dominance of China in both table tennis and badminton is so much that it has sparked fears that the sports competition may soon become "boring."

As society progressed and the economy developed, recreational sports started to permeate all levels of society. Today, about 300 million Chinese take part in sports activities regularly. More and more people consider regular sports activities to be part of their daily lives in both rural and urban areas.

Early in the morning people may be seen doing exercise. Martial arts (like Chinese boxing or swordplay) were formerly cultivated for self-defense, but they have become a form of physical exercise and are practiced in parks, streets, gardens, or on campuses now. Young and old people are also often seen jogging, playing t'ai chi ch'uan, or dancing in the parks. During the early period after the founding of the People's Republic of China, people just did aerobic exercises by using radio music during break times, and took part in spring and autumn sports meetings held each year. Nowadays, people are willing to take part in the different kinds of sports, such as table tennis, football, volleyball, and so on. Every year there are many matches played on the city-, provincial-, or national-level

competition. What's more, in recent years, some new sports, such as rock climbing, horse racing, bungee jumping, bowling, skateboarding, woman's boxing, taekwondo, and golf are becoming popular among Chinese people, especially young urban people. Sports grounds and gymnasiums have never been so busy as they are today.

中国的体育运动

Micro-video

Pingpang Match (2)

历史悠久的中国，必然会发展出一些独特的、传统的体育运动和娱乐活动。而且中国地域辽阔，各个少数民族之间相隔甚远，所以他们通过独特的体育运动来表达活力和热情不足为奇。

几乎所有的传统体育运动都起源于生产活动。蒙古族、藏族和哈萨克族人居住在辽阔的自然草原上，马术对他们的生存至关重要。因此，他们在骑马和射击方面的天赋使他们有了这些运动的形式。生活在农业区或以狩猎为生的人们则擅长攀登、摔跤、跳跃、射击等等。

许多这样的体育活动都伴随着歌唱、舞蹈和器乐表演等艺术形式。它们大多作为节日的一部分，在春节和其他重要的日子里举行。海南黎族的竹竿舞就是一个例子。持竿者双双蹲下或跪在对方的对面，两手各握一根竹竿的末端，在音乐的伴奏下，及时地将竹竿分开、合拢。优雅的舞者在移动的竹竿之间表演，确保与竹竿保持浑然一体的节奏，以免被竹竿碰到。这是一项技巧性和娱乐性兼备的活动。

有些体育活动广泛地为汉族和少数民族所共同喜爱。一般认为中国最普及的体育活动是乒乓球、羽毛球和篮球。

在国际舞台上，中国最擅长乒乓球和羽毛球等运动。事实上，中国在世界乒乓球和羽毛球领域的主导地位非常突出，以至于人们担心在这两项运动中体育竞技可能很快就会变得"乏味"了。

随着社会的进步和经济的发展，休闲体育开始渗透到社会的各个层面。今天，大约有3亿中国人定期参加体育活动。无论在农村还是城市，越来越多的人认为定期体育活动是他们日常生活的一部分。

清晨，我们可以看到人们在做各种运动。武术（像中国的拳术或剑术）以前是为了自卫而发展起来的，现在已经成为体育锻炼的一种形式，在公园、街道、花园、校园等场所屡见不鲜。年轻人和老年人也经常在公园里慢跑、打太极拳或跳舞。在中华人民共和国成立初期，人们只是在休息时间通过广播音乐做有氧运动，并参加每年举行的春秋季运动会。现在，人们愿意参加各种各样的体育运动，如乒乓球、足球、排球等。每年都有许多比赛在国家、省、市级进行。近年来兴起的一些新型体育运动，如攀岩、赛马、蹦极、保龄球、滑板、女子拳击、跆拳道、高尔夫等，在中国人民尤其是城市年轻人群中越来越流行。运动场和体育馆从来没有像现在这样繁忙过。

Exercise

Match the items in Column A with the items in Column B.

Column A	Column B
1. tug-of-war	放风筝
2. see-sawing	马术
3. walking on stilts	抽陀螺
4. whipping tops	踩高跷
5. kicking the shuttlecock	摔跤
6. kite-flying	射箭
7. wrestling	踢毽子
8. swinging	赛龙舟
9. horsemanship	跷跷板
10. archery	拔河
11. dragon-boat racing	荡秋千
12. boxing	越野跑
13. cross-country running	拳击

◎ Text B

T'ai Chi Ch'uan (Shadow Boxing)

Micro-video

Shadow Boxing

Many Chinese say that Chinese philosophy emphasizes the close relationship between physical exercises and environment. It pays more attention to inner spirit and minds. The above-mentioned two points can be seen in t'ai chi ch'uan.

T'ai chi ch'uan is one of the Chinese traditional martial arts, also know as *wushu*. Initially, it functioned as a unique and profound self-defense technique.

Boxing is complicated and basically limited within the professionals, while t'ai chi ch'uan has won wide popularity among ordinary people by its qualities of simplicity and softness. The latter adopts the principle of somatic relaxation to make people use their will, not their power, which is easy to learn and practice. That's why among all the *wushu* practitioners, t'ai chi ch'uan has the biggest numbers. The unique point of t'ai chi ch'uan is its movements. Its feature of movements is a kind of spiral winding motion that is coherent and elastic. Practitioners should be sensitive to feelings inside their body. T'ai chi ch'uan can create a flowing breath inside the body, which helps the blood run smoothly in the vessels and thus makes people more healthy.

Masters of t'ai chi ch'uan have also invented a brand-new method of practicing—hand push. Two people put their hands or spear together and keep pushing. In fact, the principle of pushing hands or spear is to use the opponent's power to attack him. More or less, it is like upfront attacking in the game of boxing.

As an typical artful Chinese kung fu, hand push has been highly popular with weak people.

Nowadays the health-care function of t'ai chi ch'uan is increasingly gaining the importance, instead of its former role. According to scientific researches, it can improve our immune system, central nervous system, and strengthen the fitness, because t'ai chi ch'uan is a practice with a perfect combination of physical movement, deep breath, and meditation. Through long years of practice, many chronic diseases can be effectively cured or relieved such as neurasthenia, insomnia, neurosis, hypertension, intestines and stomach trouble, nephrosis, arthritis, diabetes mellitus, hypochondrical, and even the obesity. So it clearly illustrates the value of t'ai chi ch'uan in disease therapy and prevention.

No matter you are young or aged, male or female, no matter strong or weak, slim or plump, you all can choose t'ai chi ch'uan as your ideal physical exercise. When practicing it quictly and slowly, you can sense the existing of air and fully enjoy the aerobic bath, meanwhile you can also feel all the movements like the rhythmically uninterrupted waves.

T'ai chi ch'uan—the world of *yin* and *yang*, the world of the nature and relaxation, will become your whole-new life style.

太极拳

许多中国人认为，中国的哲学强调体育锻炼与环境的密切关系，更加注重内在精神和思想，而这些都体现在太极拳里。

太极拳是中国传统武术之一。最初，它只是一种独特有效的自卫防御技术。

如果说拳术复杂且大多是武林高手的专利，那么太极拳则以它的简洁和柔韧赢得了广大民众的喜爱。太极拳采用全身放松、用意不用力的锻炼原则，易学易练。所以在中国练习武术的人群中，练太极拳的人数最多。太极拳的与众不同之处在于它的动作是一种螺旋式的缠绕运动，连贯而灵活，特别强调练习者对体内感觉的灵敏性。练太极的时候身体内部会产生一种流动的气息，这种气息能使血脉畅通，强身健体。

太极拳大师们还发明了一种全新的练习方法：推手，即两个人把他们的手或长矛武器放在一起，一直推。实际上，推手的练习原则是利用对手的力量去攻击对方。或多或少，就像拳击比赛中的前攻。

推手作为一种典型的充满艺术感的中国功夫，在体弱的人群中尤其受欢迎。

现在，太极拳以前的功能渐渐淡化，它的保健功能日益得到重视。根据科学研究，它可以改善我们的免疫系统、中枢神经系统，增强体质，因为太极拳是身体运动、深呼吸和冥想的完美结合。通过多年的练习，可以有效地治愈或缓解许多慢性疾病，如神经衰弱、失眠、神经症、高血压、胃肠病、肾病、关节炎、糖尿病、疑病性神经症，甚至肥胖等。这些都体现了太极拳在疾病治疗和预防中的价值。

无论男女老少，无论胖瘦强弱，所有人都可以选择太极拳作为理想的体育锻炼方式。当你安静而缓慢地练习时，你可以感受到空气的存在，并充分享受有氧的沐浴，同时你也能感受到所有的动作就如有节奏的不间断的波浪在起伏。

太极拳——阴与阳的世界，自然与放松的世界，将成为你全新的生活方式。

Exercise

Go to practice t'ai chi ch'uan and tell out your feelings after that.

Chinese Eyes on the World

American Sports

(C: Chinese　F: Foreigner)

C: It is said that in many parts of the world, there are four seasons: spring, summer, fall, and winter. In the US, however, there are only three. What does that mean?

F: Ha-ha. It means football, basketball, and baseball. That's not completely true, but almost. In every season, Americans have a ball. If you want to know what season it is, just look at what people are playing.

C: Wow. It seems that for many Americans, sports do not just occupy the sidelines. They take center court.

Extended Reading

Glolization of Sports

F: That is definitely right. Watching or attending sports events is an important part of the lives of many Americans. American life pace is very fast. People would rather to choose the sports to keep fit in their daily life. In every state of America, there are various kinds of sports, such as basketball, football, skiing, and so on.

C: Ha-ha. There are three ball games in the US.

F: Yes. Baseball is the oldest of the major American team sports. Though baseball is no longer the most popular sport, it is still referred to as the "national pastime." Also, unlike other popular spectator sports in the US, four major professional sports leagues play balls almost every day from April to October. The most popular baseball league in the US is the MLB (Major League Baseball). Baseball attracts more ticket sales than any other sport in the US, and is considered the second most popular professional sport. Baseball is also popular in many other countries, notably Japan, the Republic of Korea, and Latin American countries such as the Dominican Republic, Cuba, and Venezuela.

C: Comparing baseball—the national pastime of American, we, the Chinese, are more familiar with American basketball.

F: Football and baseball came from other old world games, while basketball was a truly American origin. Basketball was born in 1891 in Springfield, Massachusetts, when a physical education teacher James Naismith (1861–1939) hung up a couple of peach baskets on poles at opposite ends of the gymnasium and used a soccer ball to create an "indoor" sport for students during the winter. Basketball is the second most popular sport behind football. However, the NBA (National Basketball Association) is ranked third in the popularity behind football and baseball.

C: Many Chinese are familiar with NBA. We know that it is the world's premier men's professional basketball league and is one of the major professional sports leagues of North America.

F: Don't you know football? It is known as gridiron or American football outside the US and Canada. It attracts more television viewers than baseball, and is considered the most popular sport in the US.

The 32-team NFL (National Football League) is the most popular and the only major professional football league. Its championship game, the Super Bowl, is the biggest annual sporting event held in the US. Additional millions also watch college football, and some communities, particularly in rural areas, place great emphasis on their local high school teams.

C: We can see that in some American films.

Micro-video

American Basketball

Cultural Exchange

Ⅰ *Discuss the following questions with your peers.*

1. Why do people need sports?
2. How could you encourage lazy people to do more exercises?
3. Which is your favorite sport to watch?
4. What do you think are the qualities of a good team or a champion in that sport?
5. Which is more important in sport? Winning or taking part? Are you a good loser?
6. Do you know the national sports of some countries?
7. Name some sports that you like.
8. Name some sports that Chinese and Western people like. Do they have any different preferences?

Ⅱ *Fill in the blanks according to your knowledge.*

Two men are talking about NBA.

M1: There's an NBA game on TV tonight. Shall we watch it?

M2: That depends... Who's playing?

M1: The Houston Rockets and Miami Heat. You know, Yao Ming plays for the 1. ______ so we have to watch.

M2: Do you have any idea who invented basketball or the NBA? Someone must have made up the rules?

M1: I do know, yes. A 2. ______ man, 3. ______ created the game of basketball from 4. ______ original rules. It's played a little differently nowadays, but the principle is still the same.

M2: Was it first played in Canada? I'm sure I read somewhere that the first game was played in 1946 in 5. ______.

M1: That's right, the first game was between the Toronto Huskies and the New York Knickerbockers. At that time the game was pretty boring, though. They didn't introduce the 24-second clock until after 6. ______.

M2: The 24-second clock and of course an accompanying limit on the 7. ______ a team could commit in a quarter. This created the game we know and love today.

M1: So, the NBA became more and more popular after that. When it started in Canada, most children grew up playing 8. ______ and didn't really like basketball, but over the years it has changed considerably.

M2: Is the NBA one organization?

M1: Like most pro sports leagues, the NBA is a confederation of separate organizations that 9. ______ yet must also 10. ______.

M2: This kind of confederation wouldn't be able to co-survive and become more popular without outstanding leadership. By the way, how many teams are there altogether?

M1: It started out having just 11. ______ teams, but now it has 12. ______. My favorite is always the Rockets. What about yours?

Chapter 9 Movies and Films

Text Reading

Audio Material

Wolf Warrior Ⅱ

◎ *Text A*

Chinese Film: *Wolf Warrior* Ⅱ

Here was the news on *Wolf Warrior* Ⅱ in 2018: *Wolf Warrior* Ⅱ has earned more than 4.7 billion yuan (US $704 million) at the box office by August 15, which has put it on the list of top 100 global box offices. It is also the first Asian movie to enter the top 100 list, and break the monopoly of Hollywood films.

Wolf Warrior Ⅱ is described as the highest-grossing film of all time in China, and Hollywood is sitting up and taking notice.

Wolf Warrior Ⅱ has achieved unprecedented success because of its sleek production, professionally filmed fight scenes, believable storyline, and technical finesse. And by surpassing the box office collections of any Hollywood film on show in China in the past 23 years, *Wolf Warrior* Ⅱ has set a high standard for Chinese films.

Thanks to international trade rules, Hollywood movies have become the dominant force in many countries' film markets. In Asia, only Indian and Korean (ROK) movies can compete with Hollywood flicks in their respective markets. But nowadays, the success of *Wolf Warrior Ⅱ* gives us some hope of the future of Chinese films. With *Wolf Warrior Ⅱ*, we can expect domestic audiences to lap up Chinese films with high artistic values, good storylines, and professional production qualities.

The following are some of the audience's reviews.

Micro-video

Wolf Warrior Ⅱ

1. I went to watch the movie yesterday as I heard it was a big hit in China. I am not the biggest fan of Chinese movies, but this one really impressed me. I have watched *Wolf Warrior* which I would consider as a good movie, but II is much better. It is the first Chinese movie that is built on the context of African countries and actually shot in South Africa, bearing the risk of suffering the disturbance on the set. The way the plot unfolds and the courage and patriotism is delivered to its audience makes it more than a simple action movie. Love this movie and will go for a second time.

2. A terrific action flick reminiscent of classic 1990s Jackie Chan films.

3. The film's biggest draw, of course, is the Chinese action-superstar Wu Jing. As a leading man, Wu Jing is kind of a perfect package. He has not only the pretty-boy look to draw the female crowd but also a natural, convincing tough-guy persona. As an actor who has received martial arts training, he has both the physicality of Donnie Yen and the on-screen charisma of Jet Li. Most importantly, Wu Jing plays the kind of an action hero that's just all too rare these days, the one that takes just as much punishment as he dishes it. Yet he sells it with the kind of world-class commitment that is simply awe-inspiring, like Jackie Chan or Tom Cruise who repeatedly endanger themselves simply to entertain their audiences. It's all rather impressive until you realize he also has directed the movie.

4. Think less, enjoy the action.

5. Great action movie, I love it.

6. It should be the best movie of the Chinese movies I have seen. Great actors, great underwater scene, great tank drift, great theme. All my friends think it's a great movie.

7. A movie with passion.

8. Non-stop actions packed! It tops any Hollywood movie in recent years!

9. This was a well-made action movie with original action sequences that is up to par and in some parts even exceeds any Hollywood action movie we have seen during years! It appears like your everyday action flick, but as your progress it feels fresh and nothing like you have ever seen before. You are taken on a roller coaster ride from start to end, deep into some unnamed African countries.

10. The best action/war movie in Chinese movie history.

11. Non-stop actions from start to end. In my opinion, it is much better than *Final Fantasy Ⅷ*. This movie is a gem in all Chinese action movies. Wu, as a real kung fu practitioner, will definitely become a next martial art movie star after Jackie Chan.

中国电影:《战狼2》

Extended Reading

Movie *Wolf Totem*

2018年曾有这样一则关于《战狼2》的新闻:截至8月15日,《战狼2》的票房收入超过47亿元人民币(合7.04亿美元),登上全球百强票房榜。它也是第一部进入百强榜单的亚洲电影,打破了好莱坞电影的垄断地位。

《战狼2》被认为是中国有史以来票房最高的电影,甚至引起了好莱坞的关注。

《战狼2》凭借其流畅的制作、专业拍摄的打斗场景、可信的故事情节和高超的技术手段获得了空前的成功。《战狼2》的票房收入超越了过去23年里在中国上映的任何一部好莱坞电影,使中国电影成功迈上了一个新台阶。

受国际贸易规则的影响,好莱坞电影已经成为许多国家电影市场的主导力量。在亚洲,只有印度和韩国的电影能与好莱坞电影在各自的市场竞争。但是现在,《战狼2》的成功给了我们一些对中国电影未来的希望。凭借《战狼2》,我们可以期待国内观众能欣赏到艺术价值高、故事情节好和生产品质专业的中国电影。

我们来看一些观众的评论:

1. 我听说它是一部中国大片,所以昨天去看了电影。我不是中国电影最忠实的粉丝,但这部电影给我留下了深刻的印象。我曾看过《战狼》,我认为它是一部好电影,但我觉得《战狼2》更好。它是第一部背景设在非洲国家,实际上也是在南非拍摄的中国电影,在那里还要承受战乱等不安全因素的干扰风险。随着故事情节的展开,电影向观众展示的勇气和爱国主义,都远超任何一部简单的动作片电影的水准。我喜爱这部电影,还会再去看一次的。

2. 一部极好的动作片，让人想起经典的20世纪90年代的成龙电影。

3. 这部电影的最大亮点当然是中国动作巨星吴京。作为男主角，吴京非常完美。他不仅有吸引女性观众的英俊外形，同时也有天生的、令人信服的硬汉形象。作为一名受过专业武术训练的演员，他兼有甄子丹的身体素质和李连杰的银幕魅力。最重要的是，吴京饰演的动作英雄，如今已经太少见了：他惩罚别人，他也接受惩罚。然而，他以一种令人敬畏的世界级承诺来推销它，就像成龙或汤姆·克鲁斯一样：为了使观众获得享受而不断地冒险。当你意识到他也导演了这部电影，这一切就更让人印象深刻了。

4. 别想太多，享受电影。

5. 很棒的动作片，我很喜欢。

6. 这应该是我看过的中国电影中最好的一部。超级棒的演员，超级棒的水下场景，超级棒的坦克漂移，超级棒的主题。我所有的朋友都认为这是一部很棒的电影。

7. 充满激情的电影。

8. 动作一个接一个，太精彩了！超过近年来任何一部好莱坞电影。

9. 这是一部制作精良的动作电影。动作的设计都达到了标准，甚至超过了我们多年来看过的任何一部好莱坞动作电影！它起初看起来就像你看到过的其他普通动作片，但随着电影的深入，它会让你感觉不一样，仿佛你以前从未见过。你坐上了过山车，从开始到结束，深入某个不知名的非洲国家。

10. 中国电影史上最好的动作片/战争片。

11. 动作从头到尾，没有间断过。在我看来，它甚至比《最终幻想8》好看得多。这部电影是所有中国动作电影中的瑰宝。作为一名真正的功夫实践者，吴京肯定会成为继成龙之后的下一个武术电影明星。

Exercises

Ⅰ *Decide whether the following statements are TRUE or FALSE.*

1. *Wolf Warrior Ⅱ* has been put on the list of top 100 global box offices.

2. Some Chinese films have entered the top 100 list, and broken the monopoly of Hollywood films many times.

3. Romantic love is the main theme of this movie.

4. *Wolf Warrior Ⅱ* is a terrific action movie starring Jackie Chan.

5. Many people think it is the best action/war movie in Chinese movie history.

Ⅱ *Match the items in Column A with the items in Column B.*

Column A	Column B
1. news	不知名的
2. top 100	武术电影明星
3. Hollywood film	动作片电影
4. action movie	新闻
5. from start to end	100强
6. unnamed	从头至尾
7. martial art movie star	好莱坞电影

Extended Reading

New Year Movies

Ⅲ *Answer the following questions after reading the text.*

1. Have you watched *Wolf Warrior Ⅱ*? If you have, what do you think of it? If you haven't, will you go to watch it after reading Text A?

2. Have you watched any Jackie Chan's film? Why do you love it or why not?

◎*Text B*

Chinese Director Zhang Yimou

(F: Foreign student C: Chinese student)

F: I want to watch a Chinese film. Whose film is good? I mean, can you introduce one of the famous Chinese directors to me?

Expanded Link

An Interview with Zhang Yimou

C: When coming to a famous director, I have to mention Mr. Zhang Yimou.

F: Zhang Yimou? The director of *Hero*? I just saw *Hero* and I also think he is a great director.

C: Yes. Zhang Yimou has been very popular in China for more than 30 years. His recurrent theme is a celebration of the resilience, even the stubbornness, of Chinese people in the face of hardships and adversities. He is also well known for his sensitivity to color. The first movie he directed was *Red Sorghum* in 1987 which won the Golden Bear at the Berlin Film Festival. The film *Red Sorghum* is written by Mo Yan who was awarded the Nobel Prize for Literature in 2012. This movie is one of the most classical films about the Chinese people's War of Resistance Against Japan, full of dynamic edits, striking close-ups, and gorgeously photographed images.

F: Just like *Hero*, he seems to be good at making the scene magnificent, grand, and beautiful.

C: Also, in that year Zhang made another film which won the Best Film at the Chicago Film Festival and garnered an Academy Award nomination.

F: Wow. He is so great.

C: Then after a few years he made the amazing *Raise the Red Lantern* starring Gong Li.

F: I've heard of this movie.

C: In 1992 he made *The Story of Qiu Ju* about a pregnant lady. When Qiu Ju's husband was beaten up by a village director, she has to go to court again and again to find a justice. This movie is very different from his others: There is no rigid style or sumptuous photography, and it was filmed in a documentary style, which gives it a gritty look.

F: That's very different.

C: As for more recent films, in 1999 *Not One Less* won the coveted Golden Lion at the Venice Film Festival.

F: What about movies in the 2000s?

C: In 2000 he made *Happy Times* which was a socioeconomic drama, then in 2002, of course *Hero*. And in 2004, *House of Flying Daggers*, which was set in the Tang Dynasty and had a flamboyant use of color, very beautiful.

F: OK. I will go to find it.

C: In 2006 he made *Curse of the Golden Flower*, an amazing epic. It stars Gong Li, Jay Chow, and Chow Yun Fat.

F: It seems that Zhang Yimou has won many international awards.

C: Yes. Though Chinese film has a late start, it has gained a lot of achievements in the world now. Actually, there are other well-known contemporary Chinese movie directors, for example, Feng Xiaogang, Cheng Kaige, Wang Kar-wai, and Ang Lee.

F: OK, I will watch their films one by one.

中国导演张艺谋

（F:留学生　C:中国学生）

F:我想看一部中国电影。谁的电影好？我的意思是，你能给我介绍一位中国著名导演吗？

C:说到著名导演，我不得不提张艺谋先生。

F:张艺谋?《英雄》的导演？我刚看过他的《英雄》，我也认为他是一个出色的导演。

C:是的，张艺谋在中国已经走红三十多年了。中国人面对困难和逆境时的适应力和坚强是他常要表现的主题。他也以色彩的运用而闻名。1987年，他执导的第一部电影《红高粱》在柏林电影节上获得金熊奖。电影《红高粱》是根据2012年诺贝尔文学奖得主莫言的作品改编而成。这部电影是最经典的抗日战争电影之一，充满了活力的剪辑、让人难忘的特写镜头和辉煌的人物形象。

F:那就像电影《英雄》一样。他似乎很擅长拍摄宏伟、大气而美丽的场景。

C:另外，在那一年，张艺谋又拍了一部电影，这部电影在芝加哥电影节上获得了最佳影片奖，并获得了奥斯卡金像奖提名。

F:哇！他真厉害。

C:几年之后，他还导演了著名的《大红灯笼高高挂》，由巩俐主演。

F:我听说过这部电影。

C:1992年，他导演了另一部电影《秋菊打官司》，讲述的是一个孕妇因丈夫被村主任打了一顿，而不停去告状讨公道的电影。这部电影非常不同于他的其他作品:没有严格的风格或华丽的摄影，而是采用纪录片的风格，这让它看起来非常真实。

F:这个确实很不一样。

C:至于后来的电影，在1999年的威尼斯电影节上，他的《一个也不能少》获得了角逐激烈的金狮奖。

F:那在21世纪的电影事业上呢？

C:2000年，他拍摄了《幸福时光》，这是一部关于社会经济的戏剧，其后2002年当然是《英雄》。2004年的《十面埋伏》，背景设在唐朝，色彩艳丽，非常漂亮。

F:我会去找来看看。

C:2006年，他导演了《满城尽带黄金甲》，这是一部令人惊叹的史诗巨作。它由巩俐、周杰伦和周润发主演。

F:看来张艺谋已经赢得了很多国际奖项。

C:是的。虽然中国电影起步较晚，但它在世界上已取得了许多成就。实际上，我国还有其他一些著名的当代电影导演，比如冯小刚、陈凯歌、王家卫、李安。

F:好的,我会一一地去欣赏他们的电影。

Exercises

Ⅰ *Please write down the features of Zhang Yimou's films.*

Ⅱ *Can you write a movie or a person's name after each award in the following?*

奥斯卡金像奖	Academy Award/Oscar Award
最佳影片奖	Best Picture
最佳导演奖	Best Directing
最佳男主角奖	Best Actor in a Leading Role
最佳女主角奖	Best Actress in a Leading Role
最佳男配角奖	Best Actor in a Supporting Role
最佳女配角奖	Best Actress in a Supporting Role
最佳原创剧本奖	Best Original Screenplay
最佳改编剧本奖	Best Adapted Screenplay
最佳艺术指导奖	Best Art Direction/Interior or Set Decoration

Chinese Eyes on the World

Bollywood

(C: Customer looking for a DVD A: Video store assistant)

Micro-video

Bollywood

C: Just now I heard you are talking about *Dangal* and you praise the film highly.

A: Yes, it is fantastic. My sisters think it is an inspirational comedy film about women's self-determination and dignity. I think *Dangal* is a film full of humanistic care, and my daughter loves the actor Aamir Khan.

C: Is it a new Hollywood movie? It seems that I've seen all of the good Hollywood movics and now I want to try something new. Could you give me a hand to recommend, don't know what, just something different?

A: Why not try a Bollywood movie?

C: No, I've told you I've seen many

Hollywood movies. So I want something different.

A: Not Hollywood, Bollywood, Indian movie industry. *Dangal* that we were talking about just now is one of the Bollywood movies.

C: Oh, let me see.

A: Well, Bollywood, Mumbai movie industry to be exact. The name comes from a combination of Bombay (the old name for Mumbai) and Hollywood. It's becoming very popular nowadays, not just for Indians, for everyone.

C: OK. What are the characteristics of Bollywood movies?

A: They are usually musicals, based on love stories, with leading actors and actresses. There's lots of dancing too.

C: Well, that does sound different! Can you give me some more information, please?

A: Bollywood is a massive movie industry, maybe the biggest in the world. It has been going for nearly nine decades! That's a long time, but the love stories/musicals didn't become popular again until the late 1980s. The first Bollywood movies were silent. Now, the budgets for these movies are low by Hollywood standards, just like the Hong Kong movie industry. Low budget, but big success.

C: I don't think I would be too interested in the old movies. How about the new one? Love stories and musicals, you say?

A: Yes. There are lots of fun to watch. Over the years there have been about 27, 000 feature films and more being made each year.

C: It sounds like I have a massive choice. Which would you recommend? *Dangal*?

A: Well, *Dangal* is a very good choice. And the old one *Three Idiots* and the new one *Hindi Medium* are also very good and many people love these films on social problems. Anyway, be prepared for a long evening of viewing. Most Bollywood movies last for around 3 hours, but have many different elements. As I mentioned before, song and dance, love triangles, stunts, and comedy are all major parts of Bollywood movies.

C: Thanks a lot. When I watched them I'll let you know my opinion.

Cultural Exchange

Ⅰ *Please discuss the following questions in your group and then write down your answers.*

1. In your memory/opinion, what is your country's typical film plot?

2. Can you describe one of your favorite films from your homeland?
3. Which Chinese film star do you know? Can you tell us something about him/her?
4. Can you name five powerful companies in the American film industry?
5. In your country, which actor or actress is your favorite, and why?

Ⅱ *Please fill in the blanks according to your knowledge.*

Hollywood is well known by most Chinese. It's the 1. ______ capital of the world, the home of the Silver Screen.

But before Hollywood was Hollywood, it was Rancho La Brea and Rancho Los Feliz. In 1886, H. H. Wilcox bought an area of Rancho La Brea that his wife then christened "2. ______." He bought the area to make a place for rich mid-westerners to spend their winter holidays, not to 3. ______. In 1911, the Nestor Company opened Hollywood's first film studio in an old tavern on the corner of Sunset and Gower. That's how it all began.

Because of the new industry being created Hollywood would have to develop into something more than just a small community. It wasn't long before nearly all the homes along the Boulevard were replaced by 4. ______ linking the three comers since people needed to work there. Also people need to have fun there, banks, restaurants, clubs, and movie palaces sprang up during the 1920s and 1930s. They also need grand houses for the stars. At this time movie stars actually lived in Hollywood. But of course nowadays they would get mobbed everyday if they 5. ______, so they moved out to Beverly Hills.

During the 1960s, more and more businesses started to move out of Hollywood, and the nightclubs and bars moved to the west. Hollywood today is a diverse, vital, and active community striving to preserve the elegant buildings from its past.

In 1985, the Hollywood Boulevard commercial and entertainment district was officially listed in the National Register of Historic Places. This will protect the neighborhood's important buildings so that Hollywood's 6. ______ can be seen 7. ______. So when you have enough money to visit there everything will still be there, just the way it 8. ______.

Extended Reading

The Americans

Chapter 10 Social Etiquette

Text Reading

Micro-video

Table Manner (clips)

◎ *Text A*

Forms of Address

During the 1950s and 1980s in China, people loved the address "comrade" which originated in the Soviet Union and means a person who shares common aspirations with you and it was widely used as a greeting between strangers then.

In the early years of the People's Republic of China, workers were the most respected ones and they were called "*shifu* (master)." Accordingly, when the service industry developed rapidly with the social and economic development, service workers were called "*shifu*" at the beginning of the implementation of the Reform and Opening-up in China. Then Guangdong Province adopted the title of "*xiaojie* (miss)" for waitresses, female clerks, and other women in the service industry. Because it only applied to the young and pretty female attendants, it was usually taken as a compliment. With the appearance of sex services in many barber shops, hotels, and restaurants, "*xiaojie*" became the professional name for female sex workers, much to the disgust of respectable women.

Over the past few years, it has become more and more common for women in the service industries, such as, restaurant hostesses and grocery store clerks to tell their customers, "Don't call me *xiaojie*."

In the world of the officials, most of them are called by their last names and their positions. Sometimes, names are considered to emphasize the close, harmonious relationship within official circles.

People who leave the country areas to throw in labor force in the cities are now called "urban migrant workers." This is the standard form of official documents, government speeches, and the media.

Even the way that husbands address their wives has changed over time. In the past, husbands called their wives "*jiannei* (my humble wife)" or "*zhuojing* (my lowly wife)" to emphasize the lower status of women in China. Since the People's Republic of China was founded in 1949, women have become "half the sky," while men the other half, which demonstrates the equality of the sexes. It was also common for wives to be called "*airen* (my beloved)," which led many foreigners to ask why all Chinese men had "lovers." Today, men call their wives "*laopo* (my wife)." This form of address was first a very common colloquial address and now it has become a very popular form of address in both oral and written expressions.

Some traditions haven't changed at all and seem slightly incompatible with present needs.

It is an ancient Chinese moral tradition to respect one's elders. The form of address tries its best to "improve" one's age. More than ten years ago, woman who was, or seemed to be aged around 50, would tell her family with joy, "People already call me Grandma!" Nowadays, if a mature woman is called "Grandma," she will be upset and ask: "Has I already been that old?"

As a matter of fact, many Chinese people today have encountered the awkwardness of not knowing how to address others.

Micro-video

Invited or Not?

称呼问题

"同志"这称呼源于苏联，意思是拥有共同志向的人。在20世纪50—80年代的中国，"同志"被广泛地作为陌生人之间打招呼用的称呼。

在中华人民共和国成立初期，工人师傅是最受人尊敬的，他们被尊称为“师傅”。在社会经济发展过程中，服务行业迅速发展起来。在改革开放之初，服务人员大多也被称尊为“师傅”。其后，广东省开始称呼一些女服务员、女文员及其他服务业女性为“小姐”。由于这个词常常只适用于年轻漂亮的女服务员，因此，通常被看作是一种恭维。但是后来在一些理发店、酒店和餐馆里出现了“性”服务，“小姐”慢慢地成了这类女性的专属名称，为其他女性所不耻。

因此，在过去的几年里，一些服务行业的女性，比如餐厅服务员和杂货店店员会告诉他们的顾客：“不要叫我小姐。”

在公职人员的世界里，人们一般用姓加职位来称呼他们。有些时候，也会直接用他们的名字，但这常常用以强调官方圈子内的密切和谐的关系。

从农村到城市务工的人现在被称为“进城务工人员”。这是官方文件、政府演讲和媒体经常采用的标准称呼用语。

甚至丈夫称呼妻子的方式也随着时间的推移而改变。在过去，丈夫常称呼妻子为“贱内”或“拙荆”，以示女性地位的低下。自1949年中华人民共和国成立以来，妇女成了“半边天”，而男性则为另一半天，以此展示男女平等。妻子们被称为“爱人”也很常见，这导致许多外国人问为什么中国男人都有“情人”。今天，男人称呼他们的妻子为“老婆”。这种称呼本来是一个非常普通的口语化的称呼，但现在，这个称呼成为一个口头和笔头表达都很流行的称呼形式。

有些称呼习惯则由于没有改变而在现代社会面前显得有些不合时宜。

比如尊敬长辈是中国古老的道德传统。人们甚至会尽力“拔高”一个人的年龄。十多年前，一个五十岁左右的女人会高兴地告诉她的家人：“已经有人叫我奶奶了！”今天，如果一个成熟的女人被称为“奶奶”，她会不高兴地问：“我已经那么老了吗？”

事实上，现今有很多中国人都遇到过不知道如何称呼别人的尴尬情况。

Extended Reading

Giving Gifts in China

Exercises

Ⅰ *Decide whether the following statements are TRUE or FALSE.*

1. People loved the address “Mr.” and “Mrs.” after the popular address “comrade” during the 1950s and 1970s in China.

2. In China, husbands address their wives as “darling” very often.

3. Chinese men all have “lovers.”

4. Today, a mature woman is upset to be called "Grandma."

Ⅱ *Answer the following questions with what you have read.*

1. Why do women tell you "Don't call me *xiaojie*"?

2. Why did husbands call their wives "*jiannei* (my humble wife)" ?

3. In the world of the officials, those of lower ranks have a title, while those of higher ranks are simply called by their first name. Why?

4. Why is a mature woman upset when she is called "Grandma"?

◎Text B

Table Manners

The customs of taking one's seat and serving dishes play important roles in Chinese dining etiquette, especially in the banquets which are usually held in private rooms of restaurants, either for dinner or lunch. The head of the group typically enters the room first. At a formal dinner the host and key guest are seated facing each other, with the host back to the door and the main guest facing the door. Usually, guests are then seated in order of rank around the table. Guests should always wait to be guided to their places and should not sit until the host and key guest have done so. Banquets usually include four courses: *lengpan* (cold dishes), *recai* (hot dishes), *dacai* (main course, often a whole-cooked fish which symbolizes prosperity), and *tang* (soup). The serving of fruit signals the end of the meal. Even not in a banquet, but just at one's home, there are some rules to follow, for example, the diners should not sit down or begin to eat before the host (or guest of honor) has done so. When everyone is seated, the host offers to pour tea, beginning with the cup of the eldest person, and the youngest person is served last. The process is regarded as a gesture of respect for the elders.

Just as in Western cultures, communal utensils (chopsticks and spoons) are used to bring food from communal dishes to an individual's own bowl (or plate). It is considered rude and unhygienic for a diner to use his own chopsticks to pick up food from communal plates and bowls when such utensils are present.

Other potentially rude behaviors with chopsticks include playing with them, separating them in any way (such as holding one in each hand), piercing food with them, or standing them vertically in a plate of food (It is especially rude, reminding someone of images of incense or "joss" sticks used ceremoniously at funerals). A rice bowl may be lifted with one hand that scoops rice into the mouth with chopsticks. It is also considered rude to look for a favorite dish on the plate. While it is a symbol of fairness and sharing it with others to pick up eatables that are closest to the diner.

Be aware that food is shared. One of the biggest differences between Chinese and Western table manners is that in China a few dishes are placed in the center of a table and are shared by all. This means that you should feel free to help yourself not just at the beginning of the meal but throughout it as well. Also, take it as a sign of honor and offer thanks when a Chinese host takes food from the center of the table and places it on your plate.

The last piece of food on a communal dish is never served to oneself without asking for permission. When offered the last bit of food by the host or the most respected guest, it is considered rude to refuse the offer. It is regarded virtuous for diners to not leave any bit of food on their plates or bowls. Condiments, such as soy sauce or duck sauce, may not be routinely provided at high-quality restaurants. The assumption is that perfectly prepared food needs no condiments to achieve the aim that the quality of the food can be best appreciated.

When dining, Chinese people often talk and eat at the same time, which is not considered rude at all and smoking is not regarded as a taboo at the table as well. When going out with Chinese friends, they will usually try to pay the bill. They may go so far as to pay the bill on the way to the restroom or have a small fight about paying the bill. Because they only consider it polite to pay the bill when they have invited someone.

餐桌礼仪

就座和上菜顺序在中国就餐礼仪中很重要，尤其是在饭店的包间里举行的宴席。无论晚餐还是午餐，核心人物通常先进入房间。在正式的晚宴上，主人和主宾要面对面，主人背对着门，主宾面对着门。通常情况下，客人们围绕桌子按级别顺序就座。客人应该等候着被引导到他们的位置，直到主人和主宾坐好之后才能坐下。宴会的四大主菜通常包括：冷盘、热菜、大

Extended Reading

Table Manners in Different Countries

菜（通常是象征富裕的鱼）和汤。上水果标志着这顿饭的结束。即使不是在宴会上，只是在家里，有一些规则也是要遵守的。例如，用餐者不应该在主人（或贵宾）之前坐下或开始用餐。当大家就座后，主人会主动提出倒茶，从最年长的开始，最年轻的最后，以示对长者的尊重。

和西方文化一样，人们也是用公用餐具（筷子和勺子）从公用餐盘中夹菜到个人的碗或盘中。如果有公用碗盘的话，用餐者用自己的筷子从公用碗盘里夹取食物，通常被认为是不礼貌、不卫生的行为。用筷子也不应有其他一些粗鲁的行为，比如把玩筷子，以任何形式把它们分开（比如一手拿一只），用筷子扎食物，或者把它们垂直地插在一盘食物里（后者尤其应该避免，因为中国葬礼上的香都是这样竖着的）。吃饭时可以用一只手端起饭碗，另一只手用筷子把米饭送到嘴里。另外，在盘子里去翻找自己喜欢的菜，也被认为不够礼貌，应该夹起最靠近自己的食物，以体现公平及与他人分享的精神。

要知道食物是共享的。中西方餐桌礼仪最大的不同之处在于，在中国，一些菜肴被放在桌子的中间，并被所有人分享。这意味着你不仅在吃饭的开始，而且在整个过程中都可以随意地夹菜。若主人从桌子中央夹食物放在你的盘子里，那通常是非常客气的行为，你应该表示感谢。

桌上公用餐具里的最后一块食物，在未经允许的情况下，最好不要擅自夹取。当主人或最尊贵的客人把桌上最后的食物夹给你时，最好不要拒绝，你拒绝是不礼貌的。对于用餐者来说，光盘是一种美德。调味品，如酱油或鸭酱，高级餐馆里可能不会经常提供，因为一般认为完美的食物不需要调味品，这样才能最好地品尝到食物本身的味道。

吃饭的时候，中国人经常一边聊天一边吃饭，在餐桌上吸烟也不是禁忌。与中国朋友外出时，他们通常会抢着付账。他们甚至可以借去洗手间的机会买单，或者为了付账单而争吵一番。他们认为是自己请人过来的，自己付账才是礼貌的行为。

Exercises

Ⅰ *Decide whether the following statements are TRUE or FALSE.*

1. Banquets are usually held in private rooms of restraunts.
2. At a formal dinner the host and key guest are seated next to each other.
3. The serving of cakes signals the end of a meal.
4. The youngest person is served first.
5. You should feel free to help yourself throughout the meal.
6. Chinese young people are seldom chatting when having dinner.
7. In China, a few dishes are placed in the center of a table and are shared by all.
8. Chinese people will be very polite to pay the bill for their friends.

Ⅱ *Match the items in Column A with the items in Column B.*

Column A	Column B
1. host	宴席
2. guest	盘子
3. chopsticks	感谢
4. plate	主人
5. food	筷子
6. thank you	客人
7. banquet	食物

Micro-video

Table Manner

Chinese Eyes on the World

"Are You Married?"

When friends met in America they might say, "The weather is pretty fair today!" American people of different ages don't always need to be especially tactful or subtle when asked about the family situation. Asking questions point-blank is fine in certain circumstances, such as, formal situation where the person being asked is happy to divulge the information. But English people usually see these sorts of personal questions, such as marriage, and questions about children, as private and they can only talk about them in some special occasions without being offended or giving offense.

David Lamb was a reporter for the *Los Angles Times* in Vietnam and described his experience when being asked his age and marital status. He had met an ordinary young Vietnamese person on the train. As soon as the two met, the young person asked "How old are you?" In Lamb's opinion, it was one of the weirdest ways of Vietnamese to start a conversation.

Lamb had listed three questions about how Vietnamese people ask strangers, for examples, "Where are you from?" "How old are you?" and "Are you married?" The young man on the train was an exception, because after the first question, to which Lamb replied that he was 60, the young man simply asked, "How many children do you have?" Lamb replied, "I don't have any child." This prompted the young man to ask,

"Aren't you married?" Lamb said, "I'm married, but I don't have any kid." Lamb wrote, "A look of sadness swept his face, and he said 'I am very sorry for you. That's terrible. What happened? You must be lonely.'"

Lamb wrote, "As a childless husband, I was given so many expressions of sympathy to be followed by so many probing queries. My explanation of shooting blanks never seemed to clear up the issue until, eventually, I adopted a fictional family. I had two children, a boy Sebastian and a girl Aileen (names that, conveniently, the Vietnamese found difficult to pronounce), and they were back in the United States, recently married and about to start their own families. This response would elicit beaming approval from my inquisitors. 'Ah,' they'd say, 'A boy and a girl. Perfect. You are very lucky.'"

Cultural Exchange

Ⅰ *Fill in the chart below, and then share your answers with your classmates.*

In your country how do people address...	
a mother?	
a father?	
a grandfather?	
a sales clerk?	
a spouse?	
a mother-in-law?	
a boss?	
a college professor?	
a physician?	
a friend?	
a teacher?	

Ⅱ *Learn and introduce idioms.*

1. China has a long history of etiquette that is reflected in its history and stories. Here is such an example: Once upon a time, a man went on a long tour to visit his friend with a swan as a gift. But it escaped from the cage on the way and in his effort to catch it, he got hold of nothing but a feather. Instead of returning home, he continued his journey with the swan feather. When his friend received this unexpected gift, he was deeply moved by the story as well as the sincerity. Thereupon, the saying "The gift is nothing much, but it's the intention that counts" was spread far and wide. Can you tell out this idiom in Chinese?

2. Study the following Chinese idioms about social etiquette by yourselves. Tell your group members the story behind one of the idioms.

程门立雪

曾子避席

3. Can you introduce any idiom in your country with a story?

Ⅲ *For the following non-verbal and verbal behaviors in the cross-cultural interaction, mark "A" for appropriate or "I" for inappropriate.*

(　　)1. If you are a man living in an English speaking country, you must rise to your feet when a lady you know comes into the room.

(　　)2. If you want to go and see one of your English speaking friends, you can do it after lunch.

(　　)3. If you are a graduate student and meet an American professor who is a friend of your supervisor during the break in an academic conference, you can go over and have a talk with him as long as the break permits.

(　　)4. If you are invited to a dinner by one of your English speaking friends, you may bring the hostess some fruits as a present.

(　　)5.If you feel ill and therefore cannot ask your American teacher of English, you may say good-bye to him and leave immediately you have got the answer and expressed your gratitude.

(　　)6. In New York, Chen Ming called a taxi and said to the driver, "Would you mind taking me to the airport?"

(　　)7. When you are eating with an English speaking friend, you wish him "Good appetite!"

(　　)8. If you fail to understand a native speaker of English and therefore want him to repeat the utterance, you say, "I beg you pardon, please."

(　　)9. The best answer to the invitation "You really must come and see us one of these days" may be "Thanks a lot. I love meeting English people."

(　　)10. When you want to compliment John on his new coat, you can say "I like your new coat."

Chapter 11 Nonverbal Communication

Text Reading

Micro-video

Non-verbal Communication(1)

◎ *Text A*

Share It or Not?

(C: Chinese F: Foreigner)

C: Hi. Can I share some stories about my friend with you? He is really upset.

F: Sure. What's the matter?

C: Wang Liang is my best friend and he works in a Sino-German joint venture.

F: That is good.

C: One day, on his way to make a cup of coffee, he found that Wolfgang, one of his German colleagues, had seemingly put his head behind a piece of newspaper. Out of curiosity, Wang came up to Wolfgang so that he could glance at that newspaper. Then he asked, "What are you reading?"

F: Wow. Maybe something wrong...

C: But all of a sudden, Wolfgang lost his temper, he began to complain that Wang bothered him, and asked for an apology to him. Wang felt rather upset, and kept explaining that he didn't realize that his behavior was rude. After this, whenever Wolfgang sensed Wang approaching, he would soon cover up what he was reading, or stand up to keep a clear distance with Wang.

F: I can understand that since I'd been in China for a long time. I know that Chinese friends don't mind being close to each other.

C: Yes. But Wolfgang misunderstood that.

F: Don't worry too much. Actually, when I first came to China ten years ago, I was shocked by the Chinese students. I thought there were so many homosexuals in Chinese universities since students in the same gender walked hand in hand, or... oh, anyway, was very close to each other in the campus...

C: Really?

F: Yes. But then I knew that they were just very close friends. So don't worry, I'm sure that Wolfgang will know that your friend just did an apparently harmless movement accidentally.

C: I hope so.

分享？不分享？

（C:中国人　F:外国人）

C:嗨，我能和你聊聊我朋友的事吗？他真的很沮丧。

F:可以啊，他怎么了？

C:王亮是我最好的朋友，他在一家中德合资企业工作。

F:那不错嘛。

C:有一天，他在冲咖啡的时候，发现他的德国同事沃尔夫冈正在津津有味地看报纸。出于好奇，王亮靠近了沃尔夫冈，想看看他在看什么，他问："你在读什么啊？"

F:哎哟，这下可能有麻烦了……

C:沃尔夫冈突然发脾气了，开始抱怨王亮侵犯了他的隐私，并要求他道歉。王亮感到相当不安，并不断地解释说他没有意识到他的行为是不妥的。在这之后，每当沃尔夫冈发现王亮走近他时，他就会迅速盖好读物，或站起来与王亮拉开一段距离。

F:我倒很能理解，因为我在中国待过很长时间。我知道中国朋友是不介意彼此接近的。

C:是的，但是沃尔夫冈误会了这一点。

F:别担心太多。事实上，当我十年前第一次来到中国时，我也被中国学生震惊到了。我还以为中国大学里有这么多同性恋，因为同性别的学生都会手拉手，或者……哦，不管怎么说，校园里的同性学生都很亲近……

C:你真是这么认为的？

F:是的。但后来我知道他们只是非常亲密的朋友。所以不用担心，我相信沃尔夫冈会明白你朋友当时的举动明显是无心的，没有恶意的。

C:但愿如此。

Exercises

Ⅰ *Answer the following questions with what you have read in Text A.*

1. What's Wolfgang's nationality?

2. What did Wang Liang do when he found Wolfgang was reading a piece of newspaper?

4. How did Wolfgang think about Wang's behavior? Why?

5. Why did the foreigner think there were many homosexuals in China?

Ⅱ *Match the items in Column A with the items in Column B.*

Column A	Column B
1. Sino-German joint venture	好奇
2. colleagues	发脾气
3. newspaper	同事
4. curiosity	中德合资企业
5. to lose one's temper	报纸
6. to keep a clear distance with	同性恋
7. homosexuals	保持距离

◎ Text B

How Much Do You Know About Nonverbal Communication?

In the communication process, all intentional and unintentional stimuli between communicating parties, other than the spoken words, are considered to be nonverbal communication. How much meaning is conveyed by nonverbal communication? It is said to be 93%.

Micro-video
Non-verbal Communication(2)

Nonverbal communication is more believable than language and that is why Shakespeare once said: "Your lips tell me no, but there is yes, yes in your eye."

There are many types of nonverbal communication and the main categories are: facial expressions, head movements, hand and arm gestures, physical space, touching, eye contact, physical postures, and clothing.

About the meanings of nonverbal communication, some are universal, for example, facial expressions usually have the same meaning in different cultures. That is to say, when we see the facial expressions, we can usually tell out how people feel. But most of them vary from culture to culture, for example, hand gestures often have different meanings.

The differences in nonverbal communication between cultures are pretty striking. This means that when you need to communicate with people from different cultures, it makes sense to learn in advance about their nonverbal communication. This can save you a lot of embarrassment and misunderstanding. Of course, cultural stereotypes are just stereotypes, and you can't say that every individual from a different culture exhibits the same form of nonverbal communication. Still, even though individuals have a lot of international experience, they will continue to carry more or less signs of their culture of origin.

关于非语言沟通，你知道多少？

Micro-video

At Lorton

在交际过程中，除了口头表达的语言内容之外，所有交流双方有意无意的刺激都是非言语沟通。非语言沟通在人类交流过程中到底占据了多大比例？据说是93%。

非语言沟通比语言更可信，这就是为什么莎士比亚说："你的嘴巴告诉我不，但你的眼睛在说好的。"

非语言沟通有很多类型，主要有：面部表情、头部动作、手和手臂姿势、身体距离、触摸、眼神接触、身体姿势，以及服饰。

非语言沟通的含义，有少数是普遍共享的。例如，在不同的文化里，面部表情通常有相同的意思，也就是说，当我们看到对方的面部表情时，我们通常能正确说出他们的感受。但是，大多数非语言沟通因文化而异。例如，手势在不同文化里往往有不同的含义。

通常，不同文化之间非语言沟通的差异是惊人的。这意味着，当你需要与来自不同文化背景的人交流时，提前了解他们的非语言沟通方式是非常有意义的。这样可以给你省去很多尴尬和误解。当然，用某整体文化来分类的文化模板只是刻板印象，不能说每一个来自某种文化的个体都表现出同样的非语言沟通形式，但即使是拥有丰富国际经验的人，也会继续或多或少保持一些他们原生文化的特征。

Exercises

Ⅰ *Answer following the questions with what you have read in Text A.*

1. In class, the teacher is having the class while student A is smiling at the mobile phone, chatting with his girlfriend, and student B is sleeping. Do these two students have

communication with the teacher? Please explain your reason.

2. How can you understand that "... you can't say that every individual from a different culture exhibits the same form of nonverbal communication. Still, even though individuals have a lot of international experience they will continue to carry more or less signs of their culture of origin"? Can you give us an example?

Ⅱ *Please translate the following expressions into English.*

1. 非语言沟通
2. 面部表情
3. 触摸
4. 眼神接触
5. 文化差异
6. 误解

Chinese Eyes on the World

Main Categories of Nonverbal Communication

Facial Expressions

A smile is one of the most common examples of facial expressions in different cultures. While Americans smile freely at strangers, Russians regard it as strange and even impolite. In Asian cultures a smile isn't necessarily an expression of joy and friendliness but it can be used to convey a sense of pain and embarrassment. For many Scandinavians, a smile or any facial expression used to convey emotions is untypical because it is considered a weakness to show emotions.

Micro-video

Detective's Judge

Head Movements

In many cultures in the Middle East and Bulgaria, the meaning of the head movement for "Yes" is just the opposite in almost any other culture. You can imagine how confusing it can be to see somebody smile but his head movement means "No" to you. In such cases, saying "Yes" or "No" with words is enough to avoid confusion.

Hand and Arm Gestures

Hand and arm gestures as a form of nonverbal communication also widely vary among cultures. While in some cases a particular gesture means nothing to a representative of another culture, in other cases particular gestures for instance, the "thumbs-up" gesture or the "OK hand sign"—have vulgar meanings in Iran and Latin America, respectively, in other countries the "OK hand sign" means just "zero," which is not offensive.

Physical Space

The acceptable physical distance is another major cultural difference in nonverbal communication. In Latin America and the Middle East the acceptable distance is much shorter than what most Europeans and Americans feel comfortable with. This is why an American or a European might wonder why the other person is invading his personal space by standing so close, while people in other cultures might wonder why the American/European is standing so far from him (Are they trying to run away or what?).

Edward T. Hall, Father of ICC (Intercultural Communication) once said, "people regulate intimacy by controlling sensory exposure through the use of interpersonal distance and space."

So what is the proper distance for each zone? He gave four spatial zones to different relations: intimate, personal, social, and public.

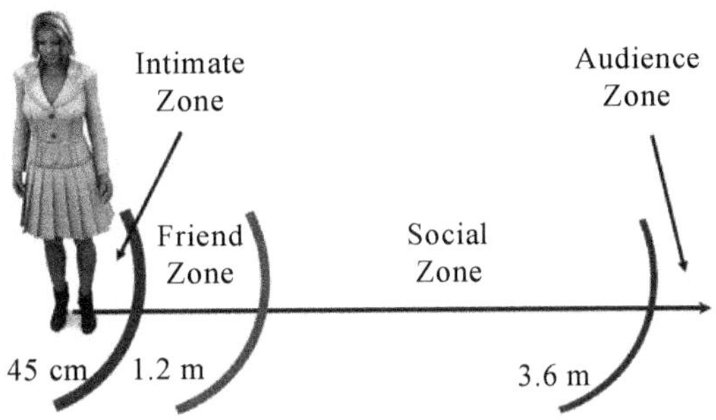

Personal Space

Touch

Touch is often used to indicate the feelings or emotions: positive or negative.

Touch is treated differently from one country to another and socially acceptable levels of touching vary from one culture to another. In the Thai culture, for example, touching someone's head may be thought of as a sense of rude. Remland and Jones studied groups of people communicating and found that touching was rare among the English (8%), the French (5%), and the Dutch (4%) compared to Italians (14%) and Greeks (12.5%). Strikingly, pushing, pulling, pinching, kicking, strangling, and hand-to-hand fighting are forms of touch in the context of physical abuse.

Middle East, Latin America, and Southern Europe are regarded as high-contact culture areas. While Asia and Northern Europe are considered to be low-contact culture areas.

As to the forms of greeting rituals, some countries use handshaking, for example, China; some countries use namaste, for example, India, and most Western countries just use one form of kissing the cheeks.

To Muslims, touch between different sexes is strictly forbidden. Same-gender touch is usually regarded as a symbol of homosexuals. In the US and Europe, there is usually no same-sex touching while they are OK with opposite-sex touching.

Micro-video

Handshake

Eye Contact

Eye contact is one of the forms of nonverbal communication where the differences are most striking. In America and Latin America not looking the other person in the eye is a sign of disrespect and it might even look suspicious ("he doesn't dare to look me in the eye, so he is hiding something"). In other cultures, for example, Asian cultures, prolonged eye contact is especially offensive, so you should avoid it at all costs.

Physical Postures

Physical postures are also quite a difference between cultures. The most common example is the habit of many American executives to rest their feet on their desks, which is considered highly offensive in Asia, the Middle East, and Europe.

Clothing

Clothing is one of the most common forms of non-verbal communication. An individual's clothing style can demonstrate his culture, mood, level of confidence, interests, age, authority, and values/beliefs. For instance, Jewish men may wear a yarmulke to outwardly communicate their religious beliefs. Similarly, clothing can communicate what nationality a person or group has, for example, in traditional festivities Scottish men often wear kilts to specify their culture.

Aside from communicating a person's beliefs and nationality, clothing can be used as a nonverbal cue to attract others. Men and women may shower themselves with accessories and high-end fashion in order to attract partners they are interested in. In this case, clothing is used as a form of self-expression that people can flaunt their power, wealth, sex appeal, or creativity. A study of the clothing worn by women attending discothèques was carried out in Vienna, Austria. It showed that in certain groups of women (especially single women), motivation for sex and levels of sexual hormones were correlated with aspects of their clothings, especially the amount of skin displayed and the presence of sheer clothing.

Cultural Exchange

Ⅰ *Answer the following questions.*

1. Have you noticed the same gesture but with different meanings in your country and in China?

2. If you are having a meeting with Americans, should you look at the speaker? Why? What about in your country?

Ⅱ *Please classify these countries into the chart.*

Norway, Italy, the Republic of Korea, Portugal, Denmark, Cuba, Malaysia, Germany, Columbia, Japan, Greece, Iran, Brazil, Thailand, Kuwait, Haiti

High-contact cultures	Low-contact cultures

Ⅲ *Fill in the chart below, and then share your answers with your classmates. In the end, perform the actions to your classmates.*

In your country what gestures do people make for...	
crazy?	
be quiet?	
goodbye?	
go away?	
come here?	
yes?	

Continued

In your country what gestures do people make for...	
no?	
stop?	
good luck?	
delicious (food)?	
everything is fine?	
I don't know?	

Ⅸ *Where do you prefer in the classroom? Can you tell out the personality traits of people who sit in different places?*

A. Front

B. Back

C. By window

D. By door

E. Middle

Chapter 12 Cultural Relics

Micro-video

The Great Wall of China

Text Reading

◎ *Text A*

The Great Wall—One of the New Seven Wonders of the World

(F: Foreign student C: Chinese student)

F: We will see the Great Wall! I am so excited because I know that the Great Wall is on the "New Seven Wonders of the World" list.

C: Yes. Today, the Great Wall is generally recognized as one of the most impressive architectural feats in history.

F: And it was built more than 2,000 years ago?

C: Yes, the construction of the Wall first began during the Warring States period about 2,500 years ago. Some kingdoms built huge walls hoping to protect their territories. When Qinshihuang, the First Emperor of China, unified China in 221 BC, he decided to have the various sections of the walls linked up and also extended. From that we got the Great Wall.

F: Is the Great Wall really ten thousand *li* long?

C: The Great Wall is also called in Chinese "*Wanli Changcheng*," which literally means "Ten Thousand *Li* Wall." Especially famous is the wall built in 220 BC–206 BC by Qinshihuang. Little of that wall remains. The Qin walls meander for about ten thousand *li*. That is the origin of the name. The Great Wall has been rebuilt, maintained, and enhanced over various dynasties; the majority of the existing wall is from the Ming Dynasty (1368–1644). A comprehensive archaeological survey, using advanced technologies, has concluded that the Ming walls measure 8,850 km (about 5,500 mi).

F: And what's the function of it?

C: The Great Wall of China was a series of fortifications made of stone, brick, tamped earth, wood, and other materials, generally built along an east-to-west line across the historical northern borders of China to protect the Chinese states and empires. The defensive characteristics of the Great Wall were enhanced by the construction of watch towers, troop barracks, garrison stations, signaling capabilities through the means of smoke or fire. Apart from defense, other purposes of the Great Wall have included border controls, allowing the imposition of duties on goods transported along the Silk Road, regulation or encouragement of trade, and the control of immigration and emigration. And the fact is that the path of the Great Wall also served as a transportation corridor.

We're approaching Badaling and you will see the Great Wall in a short while.

F: Wonderful! I've been waiting for it so long. When was the wall we are going to see built?

C: Well, the Qin Great Wall hasn't got much left today. In the subsequent dynasties, the Great Wall was rebuilt many times. The last massive rebuilding of the Great Wall was in Ming Dynasty. The Great Wall we shall see at Badaling was rebuilt then. Many western sections of the wall were constructed from mud, rather than bricks and stones, and thus were more susceptible to erosion. In 2014 a portion of the wall near the border of Liaoning and Hebei provinces was repaired with concrete. The work has been much criticized. And while portions in north of Beijing and near tourist centers have been preserved and even extensively renovated, in many other locations the Wall is in disrepair.

F: What are those towers on the wall spaced at regular distances from one another?

C: They are beacon fire tower. In ancient times, if attacked by enemies the guards would set off smoke in the day-time and bonfire at night to alarm troops stationed along the wall.

F: I see Bob and Mark are already on the wall. Let's quicken our steps.

C: Please watch your step. It's very steep here and the surface is a little slippery.

F: Now I understand why you told us to wear no high-heeled shoes.

C: Now, this is the furthest point we can go. Beyond here, the wall has not been restored yet. Why don't we sit down and rest for a while?

F: OK. This is such an amazing place! Green mountains roll over one another. Lush trees dot the slopes.

长城——“世界新七大奇迹”之一

（F:留学生　C:中国学生）

F:我们就要看到长城了，好兴奋！长城可是“世界新七大奇迹”之首啊！

C:是的。今天，长城被公认为是历史上最伟大的建筑壮举之一。

F:它是2000多年前建的吗？

C:是的，长城最早修建于约2500年前的战国时期。一些诸侯国修筑了巨大的城墙来保护他们的领地。公元前221年，秦始皇统一中国，他决定把各段城墙连接起来，并加以延长。这就是长城的由来。

Extended Reading

Seven Wonders of the World

F:长城真的有一万里吗？

C:长城又叫“万里长城”，字面意思是“绵延万里之长的城墙”。尤其著名的是中国第一位皇帝秦始皇于公元前220—前206年修建的长城。不过，那部分现在几乎没有了。秦长城蜿蜒一万余里，始有“万里长城”之称。长城在各个朝代得到重建、维护和巩固；现存长城的大部分是明朝（1368—1644）时所建。一项使用先进技术的综合考古调查得出结论，明长城全长8850千米（约5500英里）。

F:万里长城主要是用来做什么的呢？

C:中国的长城是由石头、砖块、夯土、木材和其他材料组成的一系列防御工事，大致沿着当时北方的边界线建造，以保护城墙内的州县和帝国。长城的防御特征体现在瞭望塔、兵营、驻军站、烽火台等。在古代，除国防外，长城的其他作用还包括边境管制，对沿丝绸之路运输的货物征收关税，管制或鼓励贸易，以及控制移民。此外，长城的路径也成为交通要塞。

我们快到八达岭了，你很快就会看到长城。

F:太好了！我已经迫不及待了。我们马上要看到的城墙是何时建造的呢？

C:秦长城如今已所剩无几。在秦以后的各个朝代,长城经历了多次重建。最后一次大规模的长城重建是在明朝。我们将在八达岭看到的长城就是那时重建的。西面许多的墙是用泥土建造的,而不是用砖块和石头,因此极易受到侵蚀。2014年,辽宁省和河北省交界附近的一段长城修复时用的是混凝土,招致了很多批评。虽然现在北京北部和旅游中心附近的部分城墙得到了保护,甚至是大规模的修复,但还有其他位置的城墙年久失修。

F:每隔一段城墙就有的那些塔是什么？

C:它们就是烽火台。在古代,若有敌人来袭,守台士兵会以白天燃烟、夜间点火的方式,通知驻扎在附近的警戒部队。

F:鲍勃和马克已经走到前面城墙了。我们赶快追上吧。

C:请注意脚下。这里又陡又滑。

F:我现在明白为什么你不让我们穿高跟鞋了。

C:我们最多只能走到这里了。更远的其他地方尚未修复。我们何不坐下来休息一会儿呢？

F:好。这地方真漂亮！青山层峦叠嶂,绿树点缀山冈。

Exercise

Please answer the following questions after reading the text.

1. Why is the Great Wall called the "Ten Thousand *Li* Wall"?
2. What is the function of the Great Wall?
3. What we see now is not the Great Wall built more than 2,000 years ago, why?
4. Why are the foreigners told not to wear high-heeled shoes when climbing the Great Wall?

◎ *Text B*

The Terracotta Army

Micro-video

The Terracotta Army

(C: Chinese student F: Foreign student)

C: Come back? How about your traveling in Xi'an?

F: Great. The Terracotta Army is especially impressive to me.

C: The Terracotta Army?

F: Yes. It is a super large collection of life-size terracotta sculptures in battle formations.

C: It is said that it was reproducing the mega imperial guard troops of Emperor Qinshihuang (259 BC–210 BC), the first emperor of the first unified dynasty of Imperial China.

Originally the ancient funerary project for Emperor Qinshihuang, it is now a live museum, officially named Emperor Qinshihuang's Mausoleum Site Museum, showing the life stories of the emperor and the once powerful Qin Empire (221 BC–207 BC) in those days of pomp and vigor.

F: It is amazing that there are diverse facial features of the soldiers. It is extremely difficult to find two similar figures in the three pits. Every soldier has his own facial features, which means there are thousands of different faces in total. In fact, there were only eight moulds used to make the profile of each soldier's head. The distinctive faces were carved by craftsmen individually, which definitely took massive amount of manpower. The excellent modeling skill of the Qin Dynasty artists is embodied in the vivid facial expressions created for each soldier.

C: It is said that the figures used to be colorful.

F: The figures always appear as grey in color. In fact, they were originally painted with black hair, beard, and eyebrows like real persons. Their uniforms were also painted in bright colors, including scarlet, green, black, and purple. The moist environment underground was more suited to the preservation of the paint. Once the figures were excavated, the change of the humidity led to more cracks and warping on the surface, and is the main factor resulting in the fading of the colors.

C: No wonder this enormous sculpture group amazed the world when the Xi'an Terracotta Army was discovered in 1974. The find was praised as the Eighth Wonder of the World by the former French Prime Minister Chirac early in 1978, and became a UNESCO (United Nations Educational, Scientific and Cultural Organization) World Heritage Site in 1987.

F: Yes. The pits were found to hold over 7,000 exquisite figures and horses, including burly generals, resolute military officers, and vivid soldiers. Facts from the excavation show

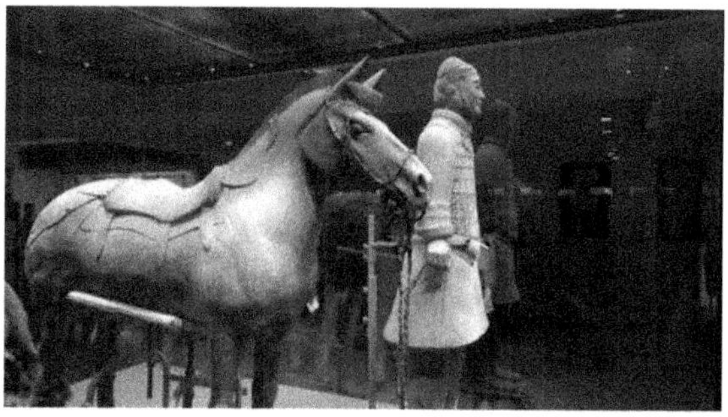

that the shortest figure of the Terracotta Army measures 70 inches (1.78 meters) in height while the tallest is over 80 inches (2 meters). The average height of all the warriors is 75 inches (1.9 meters), which is taller than modern Chinese males. Does this mean people in the olden times were much taller?

C: Not really. According to the historical fact records, the average height of males in the Qin Dynasty was around 65 inches (1.65 meters), which is very similar to the present day. The terracotta soldiers were made much taller for two reasons. On the one hand, during that period, the major form of battle was close combat, which required tall and strong warriors. On the other hand, the taller terracotta warriors are a more impressive representation of the majesty of this once dominant army.

F: What you said makes sense.

C: Being one of the most significant archeological excavations of the 20th century and a UNESCO World Heritage Site, the Terracotta Army is no doubt a must-see for every visitor to Xi'an. I will go to see it next time when I go to Xi'an.

兵马俑

(C:中国学生　F:留学生)

C:回来了？你的西安之旅怎么样？

F:很棒。特别是兵马俑给我留下了深刻的印象。

C:兵马俑吗？

F:是的。那是一大批与真人真马一样大小的按实战队形排列的兵马俑。

C:据说兵马俑的制作模仿的是中国第一个统一王朝的第一个皇帝秦始皇(公元前259—前210)的超级帝国守卫军。

最初是秦始皇的古代殡葬工程,现在是一座备受关注的博物馆,正式馆名为秦始皇帝陵博物院。它展示了这位皇帝的生前故事和昔日强大秦国(公元前221—前207)的光辉岁月。

F:令人惊奇的是,这些兵佣的面部表情千差万别。在三个坑中都很难找到两张相似的脸。每个兵俑都有自己的面部特征,这意味着总共有几千张不同的面孔。事实上,制作士兵头部的模具只有8个。这几千张独特的面孔是由工匠们单独雕刻而成的,这定是耗费了大量的人力。秦代艺术家高超的造型技巧,体现在为每个兵俑创造的生动的面部表情中。

C:据说这些俑以前是彩色的。

F:这些俑现在是灰色的。事实上,他们最初做好的时候都是像真人一样的:黑色的头发、胡须和眉毛,制服也是五颜六色的,包括红色、绿色、黑色和紫色。地下的潮湿环境更适合颜料的保存。自打这些俑被挖掘出来,湿度的变化引发了更多的裂缝和表面变形,这是导致褪色的主要因素。

C:难怪这庞大的雕塑兵马俑群1974年在西安发现时,震惊了世界。这一发现早在1978年就被法国前总理希拉克誉为世界第八大奇迹,并于1987年被联合国教科文组织列为世界文化遗产。

F:是的。坑内发现7000多个精致的兵马俑,包括魁梧的将军、坚毅的军吏和生动的士兵。考古发掘的事实表明,最矮的兵俑的高度是70英寸(约1.78米),而最高的是80英寸(约2米)。所有战士的平均身高是75英寸(约1.9米),比现代中国男性高。这是否意味着古时候的人要高得多?

C:不见得。根据史实记载,秦朝男性的平均身高约为65英寸(约1.65米),与现在非常相似。兵俑做得高了很多主要有两个方面原因:一方面,那时主要的作战形式是近距离格斗,这需要高大强壮的战士;另一方面,高大的兵马俑更能形象地展示这支曾经占统治地位的军队的威严。

F:很有道理。

C:作为20世纪最重要的考古发掘之一和联合国教科文组织认定的世界遗产,兵马俑无疑是每一个到西安的游客必看的景点。下次我去西安的时候,也要去参观。

Exercise

Match the items in Column A with the items in Column B.

Column A	Column B
1. Terracotta Army	法国前总统
2. Emperor Qinshihuang	世界第八大奇迹
3. sculpture group	秦始皇
4. the Eighth Wonder of the World	雕塑群
5. former French Prime	兵马俑
6. figure	人像

Chinese Eyes on the World

The Pyramids

(S: Student　P: Professor)

Expanded Link

解密金字塔（英文版）

S: Could you tell me about these pyramids?

P: OK. Built 4,000 years ago, the three great pyramids at Giza, in the Egyptian desert remain the most colossal buildings ever constructed. Having survived the sands of time, the pyramids rise to the number two spot on the list of the World Ten Man-made Wonders.

S: The pyramids are really one of the most impressive monuments in the ancient world.

P: Yes. They were built as tombs for the Pharaohs, the ruler of ancient Egypt. The first Pharaohs built simpler tombs, called mastaba. These mastabas were square buildings with a room inside for the coffin and the mummy and some things to take with to the afterlife.

S: Like this over here in the picture.

P: Yes. Then they began to build mounds of earth on top of their mastabas, to make them grander. Ordinary princes and other aristocrats went on being buried in mastabas. The Step Pyramid is one of the first of these new fancy tombs.

S: But, the pyramids we know all have filled in steps.

P: Yes, a short time after these were built, the Egyptians decided to fill in the steps, and then made them more pointed on top.

S: The ones in Giza are of this style, right? I think they are the most well-known and everyone in the world must have seen a picture of them.

P: Yes, the ones in Giza were built following this design. Khufu's Great Pyramid was the tallest building on earth for almost five thousand years, until the Eiffel Tower was built in 1889.

S: But you mentioned these huge buildings were constructed 4,000 years ago. How did ancient builders manage to build these massive structures? It must have called and still calls for great architectural techniques and expertise.

P: What you asked has never been fully answered but the effort clearly required brains and brawn.

S: Was there engineering genius involved?

P: Yes, there was. For example, when you're putting the block right at the top, how are you going to lug a block of stones that weighs several tons 480 feet up a structure? How are you going to do it, and how are you going to do it without leaving scratches on all the rest of the structure? And how many people does it take to drag a block weighing several tons 480 feet up into the sky? Approximately, 2.3 million blocks of stone were cut, transported, and assembled to create the Great Pyramids.

S: That's amazing! How did they build them exactly? I've heard many stories about slaves and even aliens helping them!

P: Yes, I've heard the ones about the aliens too. A pyramid is not hard to build, if you have plenty of cheap workers available. First they built a small mastaba-style tomb on the ground, in the ordinary way. Then one theory is that they heaped up tons and tons of dirt over the tomb, leaving a tunnel to the outside. Then they began placing huge stones all over the outside of the pyramid. To raise the stones to the top of the pyramid, they built long ramps of dirt and then rolled the stones up them. They kept making the ramps higher and longer. When it was done, they took the earth ramps away again. Still, it is unbelievable how they built such massive structures without machinery.

S: What was the Pharaohs' purpose to create such grandeur? Was it meant to boast the nation's power?

P: The Pharaohs may have set out to build magnificent tombs for themselves, but in the end they created monuments to human potential. There's a universal message in the pyramids. The pyramids not only belong to Egypt, but also to the world. That's why we all identify the pyramids as an early monument of human greatness.

Cultural Exchange

Ⅰ *Discuss the following questions with your peers.*

1. What are the Top 10 Man-made Wonders of the World do you think? Please explain your reasons.

2. Are there any wonders in your country? Please describe one of the wonders in your country to us.

Ⅱ *Please fill in the blanks according to your knowledge.*

(S: Chinese student P: American professor)

S: I hope that one day I can visit the Statue of Liberty and see her for real. Could you introduce some to me?

P: It was presented by the people of 1. ______ to the people of the United States in 1886 to honor the friendship between the two nations. Nowadays we consider it to be a symbol of 2. ______ throughout the world.

S: It means the America couldn't have been liberated from 3. ______ without the help of the French. Wow! It says here that more than 5 million people visit the statue every year. That's a lot of people.

P: It's a very popular symbol to many, nowhere else on earth is the concept and ideals of 4. ______ as dramatically.

S: What can you tell me about its size? How tall is it exactly?

P: The statue pan is 5. ______ feet tall and the pedestal is 6. ______ feet tall!

S: That is huge. What is it made from? It often looks like 7. ______ in the pictures.

P: Actually, the statue is made from 8. ______ coated with copper and the pedestal is made from 9. ______.

S: I see. Whom was it designed by? I guess it must have been a French designer.

P: You're right. It was designed by Frederic-Auguste Bartholdi, but the interior framework was designed by Alexandre-Gustave Eiffel, also the designer of the 10. Tower.

S: So, it was an entirely French project, then?

P: Not entirely. The pedestal was designed by an American architect, Richard Morris Hunt. But many people on both sides of the Atlantic put money into her construction.

S: Perhaps it is fitting that hundreds of thousands of ordinary people contributed hundreds of thousands of dollars to her construction and that millions more contributed millions of dollars to ensure her continued existence.

P: Yes. She may have been created by the genius of a few visionaries, but the concept she represents speaks to the hearts and minds of ordinary men and women everywhere.

Ⅲ *Read the following poem and try to answer the following questions.*

1. Where was the poet?
2. What did he see?
3. What did he think?

On the Stork Tower

by Wang Zhihuan

The sun along the mountain bows,
The Yellow River seawards flows.
You will enjoy a grander sight,
If you climb to a greater height.

Chapter 13 Education

Text Reading

Audio Material

Chinese Education

◎ *Text A*

An Introduction to Education in China

A good education has always been highly valued in China, as Chinese people believe that education ensures not only the future and development of an individual but also the progress of a family and a country as a whole. There is probably no more respectable accomplishment than a higher education.

This value can be traced back to ancient times when the maxim from *Three-Character Classic* says "If no proper education is given to children, their nature will go bad." It can be traced to the Confucian thought that "He who excels in learning can be an official." Similarly, numerous students have been convinced that "Knowledge is a pursuit above all of the others."

It has been recorded that Mencius' mother became an example to millions of mothers who longed for their children to be talented. She moved three times in order to choose a fine neighborhood that would set a positive influence on Mencius.

As far back as the Shang Dynasty (1600 BC–1046 BC), inscriptions on bones or tortoise shells were the simple records of teaching and learning. In the Western Zhou Dynasty (1046 BC–771 BC), nobles built schools to teach their children, as their offsprings would be the officials of the future, while those who were gifted but of poor families could but dream of approaching state affairs. The development of education system led to measurement that became the means by which talents would be appointed as officials in all dynasties of China. In general, this process can be divided into three periods—*chaju* and *zhengbi* in the Han Dynasty, the *jiupin zhongzheng* system from Han to the Northern and Southern Dynasties, and the Imperial Examination which survived from the Sui Dynasty (581–618) right through to the last feudal dynasty Qing Dynasty (1616–1911).

After that, China's education system fell into a state of confusion due to the changes of dynasties and war. However, with the foundation of the People's Republic of China, the new order introduced a fresh approach to education and brought it into a new phase. In long-term efforts, China's education has gained the substantial progress.

Especially since the Reform and Opening-up policy, education in China has been developing rapidly. Now in China, the education is divided into three categories: basic education, higher education, and adult education. The Compulsory Education Law stipulates that it is imperative for each child and adolescent of the right age to get a nine-year formal education.

Basic education in China includes preschool education, primary education, and general secondary education.

Preschool, or kindergarten classes, can last up to three years, when children enter as early as age three, and normally until age six, they will go to elementary school, of which the academic year is divided into two semesters.

Secondary education is divided into academic secondary education and specialized/vocational/technical secondary education.

Academic secondary education falls into academic lower and upper middle schools.

Micro-video

Fusion East & West Education

Higher education at the undergraduate level includes two- and three-year junior colleges (sometimes also called short-cycle colleges), four-year colleges, and universities offering programs in both academic and vocational subjects. Many colleges and universities also offer graduate programs leading to a master's or doctor's degree. Now part of the cost is still afforded by their families, though students can get scholarship from the college.

The classification of the adult education overlaps three sorts of education above. For example, adult primary education includes Workers' Primary Schools, Peasants' Primary Schools, and literacy classes. Adult secondary education includes radio/TV specialized secondary schools, specialized secondary schools for cadres and for staff and workers, etc.

Though great changes have taken place in the fields of education in China, there is still much to be improved.

Currently, the main problems in Chinese higher education are the growth of students' number and tuition fees. At the same time, it also faces several challenges. For example, we already know that high-quality educational resources are concentrated in big cities or several schools of those cities, while students are dispersed across the country, so the improvement of education in rural areas is a big problem. Many experts call on the government to give the poverty-stricken areas roundly of supportive measures, including the Internet and artificial intelligence used to help spread high-quality educational resources to every corner of China.

Extended Reading

Overview of Education in China

中国教育简介

在中国，良好的教育一直受到高度重视，因为中国人相信教育不仅能保证个人的未来和发展，而且能保证整个家庭和国家的发展。在中国可能没有比可以进入高等学府接受高等教育更受人尊敬的成就了。

这个价值观可以追溯到古代，如《三字经》里就说到“苟不教，性乃迁”；这也可以追溯到孔子“学而优则仕”的思想;同样,许多学子也相信“万般皆下品,唯有读书高”。史书记载的孟母是千百万母亲的榜样,但凡母亲都渴望自己的孩子有出息。为了选择一个能对孟子有好影响的好邻居,她搬了三次家。

早在商朝(公元前1600—前1046),那些甲骨文中就有教和学的简单记录。在西周时期(公元前1046—前771),贵族建造学校来教育他们的孩子,因为他们的后代将是未来的官员,而那些虽有天赋但家境贫寒的人则只能梦想着接近朝政。教育制度的发展带来了评价手段,这也成为中国历朝历代选拔官员的手段。一般来说,这个过程可分为三个阶段——在两汉是“察举制”和“征辟制”,从汉到南北朝时期为“九品中正制”,从隋朝(581—618)一直到最后一个封建王朝清朝(1616—1911)为科举制度。

此后,由于国家政权的更迭以及战乱,中国的教育体系陷入了一种混乱状态。但是,随着中华人民共和国的成立,新的秩序引入了新的教育方式,从而使中国教育进入了一个新的阶段。在长期的努力之下,中国教育已经取得了长足的发展。

特别是改革开放以来,中国教育事业发展迅速。现在在中国,教育分为三大类:基础教育、高等教育和成人教育。义务教育规定,所有适龄儿童、少年都必须接受九年的正规教育。

中国的基础教育包括学前教育、小学教育和普通中等教育。

学前教育,或者幼儿园教育,可以持续三年,儿童早在三岁就可入学,通常直到六岁时,进入小学。一学年分为两个学期。

中等教育分为普通中学和专业/职业/技术中等教育。

普通中学分为初中和高中。

大学阶段的高等教育包括两年制和三年制专科学校(有时也称为短周期学院)、四年制学院及提供学术和职业课程的大学。许多院校也提供硕士或博士学位的研究生课程。现在虽然学生也可以得到学校的奖学金,但他们的家庭还要承担其高等教育的一部分费用。

成人教育类别与以上三种类别重叠。比如成人初等教育包括工人小学、农民小学和扫盲班。成人中等教育包括广播电视中等专业学校和干部、职工中等专业学校等。

虽然中国的教育领域发生了巨大的变化,但仍有许多有待改进的地方。

目前,我国高等教育的主要问题是学生数量和学费的增长。同时,它也面临着一些其他方面的挑战,比如鉴于优质教育资源集中在大城市或这些大城市的几所学校,而学生则分散在全国各地,农村教育质量的提高是个大问题。许多专家呼吁政府向贫困地区提供全方位的扶持措施,包括互联网和人工智能,从而将优质教育资源传播到中国的每一个角落。

Exercise

Decide whether the following statements are TRUE or FALSE.

1. "If no proper education is given to children, their nature will go bad" was said by Confucius.

2. Imperial Examination began in the last feudal dynasty Qing Dynasty (1644–1911).

3. Chinese education is divided into four categories.

4. Basic education in China includes preschool education, primary education, and regular secondary education.

5. In China, each child can have any years of formal education as he wants.

6. Quality education resources are concentrated in rural areas.

◎ *Text B*

English Learning in China

(F: Foreigner C: Chinese)

F: I have found that Chinese people, especially many young people are good at English, and what's more, they all have a strong desire to learn English well. I'm very impressed by this.

C: Many friends of mine are striving to learn English well since English has become one of the most favorable skills of human resources managers.

F: Only university students make great efforts to learn English?

C: No. Many Chinese are learning English including children, adolescents, and adults. Some learn English at school, some by themselves, and others through radio, television, and films. For Chinese, one must work hard to master a foreign language.

F: What motivates them to learn English?

C: It is difficult to answer this question. In the past many boys and girls learned English at school just because it was one of their subjects, just as Chinese and maths. Then, thanks to China's Reform and Opening-up policy, the Belt and Road Initiative, and other policies, English is becoming more and more important in people's life. Many people keep learning English for their higher studies, because at colleges or universities some of their books are in English. Some people learn English just because they have to use English in their work. Other people learn English because they want to read English newspapers and magazines.

F: Oh, I see that learning English well will give us a good future. It will allow us to reach out to a world of knowledge and technologies, and make the best use of these.

C: That's true. We also learn English so that we can communicate easily with each other in the internationalized world, and learn from each other's cultures.

F: When do Chinese people usually start to learn English?

C: Usually, they learn English when they are at the kindergarten. They not only study English in school, but also take various training courses to learn English. All our primary school students are now learning English. And there is a demand for English language training among those who have already graduated—either because they did not have a chance to learn the language earlier or because they are trying to improve their English.

F: Wow, Chinese people pay really high attention to English.

C: In 10–15 years, Chinese students will leave school with a reasonable English competence. They will be able to interact more freely and comfortably with foreigners. It will bring them a new competitive advantage.

F: Looking at so many college students preparing for CET-4 or CET-6, I am sure you will achieve your goals.

中国的英语学习

(F:外国人　C:中国人)

F:我发现中国人,尤其是很多年轻人都很擅长英语,而且他们都很想学好英语。我对此印象深刻。

C:我的许多朋友都在努力学习英语,因为英语已经是公司人力资源经理招聘时最青睐的技能之一。

F:只有大学生会特别努力学习英语吗?

C:不是的。在中国,很多人,无论儿童、青少年还是成人都在学英语。有些人在学校里学，有些人自学，有些人通过广播、电视、电影学。对中国人来说，掌握一门外语是要下苦功夫的。

F：他们为什么有这么大的动力？

C：这个问题很难回答。过去，学生在学校学英语只是因为它是一门课程，就跟语文和数学一样……后来，由于中国的改革开放政策、"一带一路"倡议等，英语在人们的生活中越来越重要。有些人不断学习英语是为了深造，因为在大学里，有些课本是英文的；有些人学习英语只是因为他们的工作必须使用英语；还有些人学习英语是因为他们想读英文报纸和杂志。

F：确实，学好英语，我们就能够运用英语接触到更多的知识和技术，并充分利用这些知识和技术。

C：是的。我们学习英语还有一个目的，就是希望能在国际化世界里彼此轻松沟通，学习对方的文化。

F：中国人一般什么时候开始学英语？

C：通常是在幼儿园的时候。他们不仅在学校学，还参加各种培训班。现在所有的小学生都在学英语。毕业之后的学生也有对英语语言培训的需求，要么是因为他们没有机会更早地学习英语，要么是因为他们想要提高英语水平。

F：哇，中国人对英语真是高度重视。

C：在未来10—15年的时间里，中国学生将会以相当好的英语水平离开学校。他们将更自由自在地与外国人交流。这将给他们带来新的竞争优势。

F：看到这么多大学生正在准备大学英语四级或六级考试，我相信你们会实现目标的。

Exercise

Answer the following questions after you have read Text B.

1. How do you understand the popularity of English learning?

2. What is your advice to Chinese on English learning?

3. Read the following report and compare with the Chinese popularity of English learning. Can you analyze why the two countries have such different phenomena?

British teenagers are trapped in a vicious circle of "monolingualism." English youngsters are among the worst in Europe at foreign languages.

Teenagers in 14 different European countries were tested on their ability to speak the first foreign language taught in schools, which for UK was French. In reading, writing, and listening tests, British pupils were ranked bottom.

Youngsters are lagging far behind their European peers, with many unable to understand more than basic words or phrases. Just 11 percent of English pupils studying French were considered "independent users" in writing.

Chinese Eyes on the World

Montessori Education & Waldorf Education

Montessori Education

Montessori education is an educational approach developed by Italian physician and educator Maria Montessori.

In 1907 Montessori founded the Children's Home in the favelas of Rome. She enrolled children aged 3 to 6 and tried education. She used her original method to teach. Those ordinary, poor children, after a few years, had undergone a great mental transformation, and was trained to be bright, confident, educated, and dynamic young talents. Montessori's new method of teaching, with its huge education appeal, has caused a stir throughout Europe, with "reports of these wonderful children spreading like wildfire." Many new children's homes have been built in the style of Montessori since then.

Now Montessori education is practiced in an estimated 7,000 schools worldwide, serving children from birth to 18 years old. There are also many training institutions in China.

Montessori education is characterized by an emphasis on independence, freedom within limits, and respect for a child's natural psychological development. Although a range of practices exists under the name Montessori, the Association Montessori Internationale (AMI) and the American Montessori Society (AMS) cite these elements as essential:

1. Mixed age classrooms, with classrooms for children aged from 2.5 or 3 to 6 years old by far the most common.
2. Students' choice of activity from within a prescribed range of options.
3. Uninterrupted blocks of work time.
4. A constructivist or "discovery" model, where students learn concepts from working with materials, rather than by direct instruction.

5. Specialized educational materials developed by Montessori and her collaborators.

Waldorf Education

Waldorf education, also known as Steiner education, is a humanistic approach to pedagogy based on the educational philosophy of the Austrian philosopher Rudolf Steiner, the founder of anthroposophy. The first Waldorf school was founded in 1919 in Stuttgart, Germany. At present there are 1, 026 independent Waldorf schools, 2, 000 kindergartens, and 646 centers for special education, located in 60 countries. There are also Waldorf-based public (state) schools, charter schools, and homeschool environments.

Waldorf pedagogy distinguishes three broad stages in child development, each lasting approximately seven years. The early years education focuses on providing practical, hands-on activities and environments that encourage creative play. In the elementary school, the emphasis is on developing pupils' artistic expression and social capacities, fostering both creative and analytical modes of understanding. Secondary education focuses on developing critical understanding and fostering idealism. Throughout, the approach stresses the role of the imagination in learning and places a strong value on integrating academic, practical, and artistic pursuits.

The educational philosophy's overarching goals are intended to provide young people the basis upon which integrated individuals are equipped with a high degree of social competence. Teachers generally use formative (qualitative) rather than summative (quantitative) assessment methods, particularly in the pre-adolescent years. The schools have a high degree of autonomy to decide how best to construct their curricula and govern themselves.

The teaching methods in Waldorf are very special. The most striking feature is that

there is an organic agricultural garden in every Waldorf school or kindergarten, with different conditions and sizes. The concomitant of the organic agricultural garden is the agricultural garden classrooms. Like ordinary classrooms, there are blackboards, desks, and chairs. The difference is that there are also kitchen utensils and tableware in the garden classroom.

Cultural Exchange

Ⅰ *Fill in the chart, and then share your answers with your classmates.*

Concerning school in your country...	
at what age does a child start school?	
how many years are required?	
is primary education free? If not, how much?	
is physical punishment allowed?	
do students wear uniform?	
how much homework is given?	
is questioning of teachers encouraged?	
is it all right for a student to copy someone else's work or copy from the book?	
how is it determined as to who goes to college?	

Ⅱ *Discuss the following questions with your peers.*

1. What are the common teaching methods in your country?
2. What teaching methods are common in China?
3. Can you use the same teaching method for teaching different subjects?
4. Is rote memorization an effective way for studying?
5. Is it important to teach students about real world issues?
6. What are the advantages of co-educational learning? And what are the disadvantages?
7. What are the advantages of single-sex schools? And what are the disadvantages?
8. Is it important to be objective when teaching?
9. Some people say "Those who can, work. Those who can't, teach." What do you think of this quote?
10. Is it important for students to have a well-rounded education?

11. Is there too much emphasis put on one field of studies in China?

12. Does Chinese education adequately prepare students for the real world?

13. Are standardized tests a far way to assess a student's abilities?

14. Is it fair to pay teachers based on their students' performance?

15. Is teaching a respectable career in China?

16. What are some issues with the Chinese education system?

17. Is there too much pressure placed on students to do well in school in your hometown? Where does this pressure come from?

Ⅲ *Continue the conversation.*

Work in pairs. One person acts as an elementary school teacher, Mr. Roberts, and the other a parent (father/mother) of any one of the students listed below. The parent calls Mr. Roberts and asks him to give a progress report on the child. Begin as in the example below. Use the information provided and your imagination to continue the conversation.

MRS. BAKER: Hello, Mr. Roberts. This is Mrs. Baker, Lino's mother. Can you please tell me how my son is doing?

MRs. ROBERTS: Mrs. Baker, Lino is doing very well in math, but...

Name of student	Behavior	Reading	Math	Social Studies
Melissa Costa	talking too much	B	B^+	A
Lino Baker	troublemaker	D	A	C
Corie Espinoza	perfect	A	A	A
Tony Cobb	disinterested	D	D	F
Jasmine Choy	obedient	C^-	D	C^-
Eric Miller	often absent or late	C	C	C

Chapter 14 Values and Beliefs

Text Reading

Micro-video

Chinese Values & Beliefs (1)

◎ *Text A*

Chinese Values and Beliefs

Long History

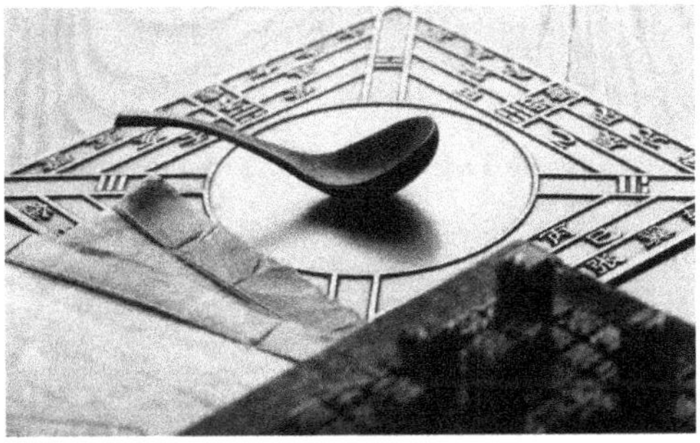

The Chinese take pride in the 5,000 years of history and rich experiences in creating important cornerstones for civilization. Just a few of the listed inventions that originate from China include: paper-making, gunpowder, silk, magnetic compass, abacus, ink, wheelbarrow, Chinese chess, tea, paper money, seismograph, kite, umbrella, etc. By contrast, the Chinese view the US as a relatively "new" country with a short history of only more than 200 years.

Confucianism

Confucianism is a part of the ancient tradition upon which Chinese culture is derived. There are four basic virtues that are considered the cornerstones of this philosophy, which are loyalty, filial piety, benevolence, and righteousness.

***Mianzi* (Face)**

The idea of shame, which is usually expressed as "face," could be loosely defined as the "status" or "self-respect" in Chinese and is by no means alien to foreigners. It is the worst thing for a Chinese to "lose face." Never insult, embarrass, shame, yell at or demean a person, since all these actions would risk putting a Chinese in a situation that he might lose face. Don't try to prove someone wrong or shout at him in public. In order to get a successful effect without making a Chinese "lose face," any criticism should be delivered privately, discreetly and tactfully, or else, it would be just opposite to what you wish.

Guanxi **(Interpersonal Relationship)**

Throughout much of Chinese history, the cohesive force that has held society together is the concept of *guanxi*, i.e., interpersonal relationship. It is very important for the Chinese to have good relationships. They often regard good social relations as a symbol of personal ability and influence.

Keqi

Keqi not only means thoughtfulness, politeness, and courtesy, but also represents humbleness and modesty. It is impolite to be arrogant and brag about oneself or people on one's own side. The expression is most often used in the negative version, as in "*buyao keqi*," meaning "you shouldn't be so distant and polite to me" or "you're welcome."

Roundabout Ways

Seldom do Chinese express what they think directly, nor will they show their emotions and feelings in public. In contrast to the more direct expressions of feelings in greeting or farewell among westerners, such as hugging or kissing, Chinese people usually greet others with a simple handshake in daily life.

Perseverance

An ancient Chinese viewpoint is always passed on from older generation to younger generation: "With time and patience, the mulberry leaf becomes a silk gown."

Colors and Numbers

Red is considered a symbol of celebration and is deemed lucky or fortunate. Pink and yellow typically mean prosperity. White, gray, and black stand for funeral.

The Chinese selection of lucky numbers is often based on the sound. For example, the number eight (8) is associated with "prosperity" because the sound is similar to the Chinese word "*fa* (prosperity)" and is desirable for all occasions. The number nine (9) is associated with "eternal" and is welcomed by all now, even though originally it could only be used by the imperial family. The Forbidden City, for example, was designed with

9, 999 rooms. The number six (6) represents good luck and can also reflect the six elements of nature—wind, mountains, rivers, light, the moon, and the sun. The number four (4) sounds like "death" in Chinese, so some buildings will often skip the fourth floor.

Micro-video

Chinese Values & Beliefs (2)

To sum up, do in Rome as the Romans do, but you need not worry about these cultural barriers because most Chinese are hospitable and amiable and will not mind your nonproficiency.

中国人的价值理念

Extended Reading

Exchange of Gifts

悠久的历史

中国人对其5000年的悠久历史和文明引以为豪,他们为世界文明做出了重要贡献。源自中国的发明数不胜数,比如造纸术、火药、丝绸、磁罗盘、算盘、墨水、独轮车、象棋、茶叶、纸币、地震仪、风筝和雨伞等。相比之下,中国人认为,美国是一个相对"新"的国家,因为它只有短短200多年的历史。

儒家思想

儒家思想作为古老的传统,是中国文化的起源之一,此哲学思想强调的四种基本美德被视为其基石,它们是:忠、孝、仁、义。

面子(脸)

羞耻感这个概念通常被表达为"面子(脸)",可以宽泛地定义为"地位"或"自尊",外国人对此并不陌生。对中国人来说,丢脸是最糟糕的事情。绝不要辱骂、捉弄、羞辱、吼叫或贬低一个人。因为所有这些行为都有可能使中国人陷入失去面子的境地。不要试图证明某人是错误的,也不要在公共场合对他大喊大叫。一般来说为了取得理想的效果,不使中国人丢脸,批评都应该私下进行,谨慎而又要充满智慧,否则将事与愿违。

关系(人际关系)

纵观中国的历史,把社会连接起来的一直是关系,即人与人之间的关系。对于中国人来说,拥有良好的人际关系是非常重要的,他们通常视良好的社会关系为个人能力和影响力的象征。

客气

"客气"不仅意味着体贴、礼貌、礼节,也代表谦逊。傲慢自大、吹嘘自己或自己人是不礼貌的。这个表达最常被用在否定句中,如"不要客气",意思是"你不应该对我那么礼貌(生分)"或"随便点"。

迂回表达

中国人很少直接表达自己的想法，而喜欢采用迂回的表达方式。在公共场合也不太表露自己的情绪和感受。与西方人问候或道别时的更直接的情感表达（比如拥抱或亲吻）不同，中国人在日常生活中通常用握手来问候他人。

恒心

有一个古老的中国观念代代相传：只要功夫深，铁杵磨成针。

颜色和数字

红色被认为是喜庆的颜色，也被认为是幸运的颜色。粉色和黄色代表繁荣。白色、灰色和黑色是葬礼的颜色。

中国人对幸运数字的选择多是基于发音。例如，在汉语中，8与"发"相似，适合所有场合。9因为发音让人联想到"永久"而被人喜爱。最初它只能被皇室使用，比如紫禁城设计有9999个房间。6代表好运，也能反映大自然的六大元素——风、山、河、光、月、日。数字4在汉语中听起来像"死"，因此高楼常不设四楼。

总之，入乡随俗，但你不必担心这些文化障碍，因为大多数中国人都是热情好客的，如果你一个外国人因为不了解习俗而做了不符合习俗的事情，他们通常也不会放在心上或责怪你的。

Exercises

Ⅰ *Decide whether the following statements are TRUE or FALSE.*

1. There are four basic virtues that are considered the cornerstones of Confucianism: loyalty, filial piety, benevolence, and righteousness.

2. Any criticism is supposed to be delivered privately because people don't want to "lose face."

3. Few people in China regard good social relations as a symbol of personal ability and influence.

4. The Chinese will express what they think directly.

5. The number nine (9) is associated with "prosperity" and is desirable for all occasions.

6. The Chinese will be not happy if you do something wrong due to your nonproficiency in Chinese customs.

Ⅱ *Discuss the following questions with your peers.*

Read the following dialogue between a British teacher (T) and a Chinese student (S) and share your understanding of what the student wants to say.

T: Yes?

S: Ms. Bowmen?

T: What is it?

S: My mother is ill...

T: And?

S: She has to go to hospital...

T: What do you want? I am very busy and I can't follow you.

S: Nothing. Ms.

Ⅲ *Read the following short case and answer the questions.*

Case: Thank you! I will try!

A Chinese researcher, visiting America, was invited by his supervisor to dinner at home. He kept saying "Thank you" and "I will try to come" all the time. This irritated his American supervisor who wanted a simple "yes" or "no." He had no idea whether the Chinese has accepted his invitation or not.

Questions:

1. What does the researcher mean by saying "I will try" in the Chinese way?
2. Why was the supervisor irritated?
3. What is the typical answer in your culture?

◎ *Text B*

Confucius

(F: Foreign student C: Chinese professor)

F: When coming to Chinese values and beliefs, is there anybody in the history who has a very great impact on it?

C: It goes without saying that Confucius' impact on the Chinese is the greatest. Throughout history, Confucius is widely considered one of the most important and influential individuals in affecting the lives of humanity. His philosophy greatly impacted people around the world and is still lingering in today's society.

F: Confucius must be a great philosopher.

C: Confucius is not only a great philosopher, but also an educator, a politician, as well as the founder of Confucianism, which still has a tremendous influence over people today.

F: A great man!

C: Confucianism is the backbone of traditional Chinese culture. Confucius developed his philosophy around the concept of benevolence. *The Analects of Confucius* demonstrates his political views, ethics thoughts, moral ideas, and pedagogical principles. Confucianism represents a set of moral principles because it stresses fairness and harmony in human relationships, as well as the individual's social responsibility for their country. For Confucius, political honesty is based on individual ethical integrity.

F: What is the core of Confucianism?

C: With particular emphasis on the importance of the family and social harmony, rather than on an otherworldly source of spiritual values, the core of Confucianism is humanistic. The worldly concern of Confucianism rests upon the belief that human beings are fundamentally good, and teachable, improvable, and perfectible through personal and communal endeavors especially self-cultivation and self-creation. Confucianism focuses on the cultivation of virtue in an ethical world. Some of the basic Confucian ethical concepts and practices include *ren*, *yi*, *li*, and *zhi*. *Ren*, "benevolence" or "humaneness," is the essence of the human being, which is manifested as compassion. *Yi* is the upholding of righteousness and the moral disposition of showing mercy. *Li* is a system of ritual norms and propriety, which determines how a person should act properly in everyday life. *Zhi* is the ability to tell what is right and fair, or the converse, in the behaviors exhibited by others.

F: Great! I remember that some American scholars did a comparative study of Confucius with ancient Greek and Roman philosophers. Their conclusion was that there is more practical value in Confucianism. Do you know the reason?

C: With the rise of individualism in the community becoming a serious threat to social harmony and progress, a different set of values is needed as a counterbalance. Since Confucianism emphasizes "courtesy" and "respect" when dealing with people or nature, it should be very beneficial for building harmony in any society as a result. The

other reason may be that Confucius was also an accomplished educator. He treated his students equally by teaching them democratic and open-minded ideas. In the words of the American scholars, Confucius wanted to train his students to become more unrestrained and adaptable to external influences.

F: Yeah, very reasonable. I will go to study Confucius.

C: More and more Chinese students are studying *The Analects of Confucius*. Some companies are even using Confucianism as a management tool now. The government is also promoting the Confucian values of ethics, fairness, and honesty. They see it as a way to address the social problems that have emerged as a result of the accelerated economic growth.

孔 子

（F:留学生　C:中国教授）

F:说起中国的价值理念,历史上对此影响最大的要算哪位呢?

C:当然是孔子对中国人的影响最大。纵观历史,孔子被广泛认为是影响人类生活的最重要、最具影响力的人物之一。他的哲学观点曾对世界各地的人们产生过巨大的影响,对当今社会仍有着不可忽视的影响力。

F:孔子一定是个伟大的哲学家。

C:孔子不仅是一位伟大的哲学家,也是一位教育家、政治家,是儒家思想的创始人。他所创建的儒家思想至今仍对人们产生巨大的影响。

F:真了不起!

C:儒家思想是中国传统文化的支柱。孔子的哲学体系是以“仁”为基础的,《论语》集中体现了他的政治主张、伦理思想、道德观念及教育原则等。儒家思想是一套伦理道德体系,强调的是为人处世的正派、人际关系的和谐以及个人对国家的责任感。在孔子看来,政治上的正直是以人品的正直为基础的。

F:儒家思想的核心是什么?

C:儒家思想尤其强调家庭和社会和谐的重要性,而不是来世的精神价值,它的核心是以人为本。儒家的世俗关怀依赖于一种信念,即人从根本上是善的、可教的、可改善的,并且是通过个人和集体的努力,特别是自我修养和自我创造来实现的。儒家思想注重在道德世界中培养美德。基本的儒家伦理观念和实践包括仁、义、礼和智。仁,即仁爱、慈悲,是人类的本质,表现为同情。义,是指正义和道义。礼,即礼仪和礼节,决定了一个人在日常生活中应该有适当的行为。智,是指辨别是非、明善恶的能力。

F:很厉害。我记得有一些美国学者对孔子和古希腊、古罗马哲学家进行了比较研究。他们的结论是,儒家思想具有更大的实用价值。你知道原因吗?

C:个人主义在社会上的兴起,对社会和谐和进步构成了严重威胁,因此需要一套不同的价值观作为平衡。儒家思想在与人或自然打交道时强调"礼"和"敬",这对任何社会的和谐都是非常有益的。另一个原因可能是孔子还是位了不起的教育家,他平等对待学生,教给他们民主、开放的观念。用美国学者的话说就是:孔子要培养的是能够自然、从容并适应环境的君子。

F:是的,非常有道理。我要去研究一下孔子。

C:越来越多的中国学生正在学习《论语》。如今一些公司甚至将儒家思想作为管理工具。政府也在提倡儒家的道德、公平和诚实的价值观。他们认为这是解决由于经济加速增长而出现的社会问题的一种方式。

Exercises

Ⅰ *Please answer the following question after reading the text.*

What do you think of Confucius' thoughts?

Micro-video

Business Values

Ⅱ *Match the items in Column A with the items in Column B.*

Column A	Column B
1. Confucius	人本主义
2. philosopher	孔子
3. educator	儒家思想
4. politician	哲学家
5. Confucianism	教育家
6. humanistic	政治家
7. courtesy	敬
8. respect	礼

Chinese Eyes on the World

Americans Morals

Do Americans have any morals? That's a good question. Many people insist that

ideas about right and wrong are merely personal opinions. Some voices, though, are calling Americans back to traditional moral values. William J. Bennett, former US Secretary of Education, edited *The Book of Virtues* in 1993 to do just that. Bennett suggests that great moral stories can build character. The success of Bennett's book shows that many Americans still believe in moral values. But what are they?

To begin with, moral values in America are like those in any culture. In fact, many aspects of morality are universal. But the stories and traditions that teach them are unique to each culture. Not only that, but culture influences how people show these virtues.

One of the most basic moral values for Americans is honesty. The well-known legend about George Washington and the cherry tree teaches us this value clearly. Little George cut down his father's favorite cherry tree when trying out his new hatchet. When his father asked him about it, George said, "I cannot tell a lie. I did it with my hatchet." Instead of punishment, George received praise for telling the truth. Sometimes American "honesty"—being open and direct—might offend people. But Americans still believe that "Honesty is the best policy."

Another virtue Americans "respect" is perseverance. Do you remember one of *Aesop's Fables* about the race between a hare and a turtoise? The hare thought he could win easily, so he took a nap. But it was the turtoise that finally won because he did not give up. Another story tells about a little train climbing a steep hill. The hill was so steep that the little train had a hard time trying to get over it. But the train just kept pulling, all the while saying to himself, "I think I can. I think I can." At last, the train was over the top of the hill. "I thought I could, I thought I could," chugged the happy little train.

Compassion may be the queen of American virtues. The story of "The Good Samaritan" from the Bible describes a man who showed compassion. On his way to some cities, a Samaritan found a poor traveler lying on the road. The traveler had been beaten and robbed. The kind Samaritan, instead of just passing by, stopped to help this person in need. Compassion can even turn into a positive cycle. In the fall of 1992, people in Iowa sent truckloads of water to help Floridians who had been hit by a hurricane. The next summer, during the Midwest flooding, Florida returned the favor. In less dramatic ways, millions of Americans are quietly passing along the kindnesses shown to them.

In no way can this brief description cover all the moral values honored by Americans. Courage, responsibility, loyalty, gratitude, and any others could be discussed. In fact, Bennett's bestseller—over 800 pages—highlights just 10 virtues. Even Bennett admits that he has only scratched the surface. But no matter how long or short the list is, moral values are invaluable. They are the foundation of American culture and any culture.

Micro-video

Western View of Sex

Cultural Exchange

Ⅰ *Fill in the chart, and then share your answers with your classmates.*

When it comes to aging in your country...	
is it acceptable to ask people their age?	
at what age do people retire?	
at what age are people considered old?	
do people try to slow the effects of aging? If so, how? (Hair dyeing? Surgery? Else?)	
what are the privileges of aging? (Discounted prices? Respect? Else?)	

Ⅱ *Discuss the following questions with your classmates.*

1. In your culture, do you celebrate birthdays? Which birthdays are the most special ones?

2. In your culture, where do the elderly live and with whom?

3. In your culture, does one particular child take care of the elderly parents, or do all the children share the responsibility?

4. In your culture, are elderly men treated the same as elderly women? Explain in detail.

5. How are the attitudes towards the elderly and aging in the US the same as or different from those in your country?

6. What do you see as the disadvantages of getting old in the US compared to that in your country? Do you see any advantages?

Ⅲ *Play a game.*

Values and beliefs are really the sources of our life. We all know that pain and pleasure is the driving force of our behavior. We learn to give labels for different kinds of pain and pleasure throughout our lives. Those labels are what we call values.

Every one of us has two types of values: moving-towards values and moving-away-from values.

Ask yourself the question: What's the most important to me in ______? And make a list.

Moving-towards values:

1) success

2) adventure

3) health

4) security

5) passion

6) growth

7) love

8) contribution

Which one would you do the most to avoid?

Moving-away-from values:

1) anger

2) frustration

3) depression

4) humiliation

5) physical pain

Do you have conflicts there? For example, your No. 1 moving-towards value is success, but health is not on your list. Can you really be successful without health? Or your No. 1 moving-towards value is success, but your No. 1 moving-away-from value is pain of rejection. Can these two go together? You'd better believe it doesn't.

Your values determine what you will focus on. If you change your values, you change your destiny. If you don't change your values, you should at least adapt your rules to these values. For me every day alive is a great day. Don't make the rules too tough for you to win the game of life.

Ⅳ *Read the case of "No. She is from Africa!" and then discuss questions with your Chinese friends or teachers.*

Case: No. She is from Africa!

Mr. Golles works for an international company in China.

Once he commented on his secretary with his Chinese colleague, Li Fei. "I think Dobbie devoted herself to the post. She is a really white person." "A white person?" Li Fei was surprised, "No. She is from Africa!"

Discuss the following questions with your Chinese friends or teachers:

1. Can you find any conflict in this case?

2. How do you understand the "white person" here?

Chapter 15 Reform and Opening-up

Text Reading

◎ *Text A*

Reform and Opening-up Policy in China

(F: Foreign student C: Chinese professor)

F: When coming to China, we see an up-and-coming, dynamic, and rapidly developing country whose economic strength has met a global benchmark. Some Chinese cutting-edge technologies are gradually occupying the world market, Chinese consumer goods have become an integral part of the world's shopping centers, and Chinese travelers are also dominating the tourism industry. However, my father who came here 20 years ago told me about a different China before I came.

C: What seems to be quite natural today was hardly conceivable not so long ago.

F: Why?

C: China's prosperity today owes much to the reform and opening-up policy.

F: What is the reform and opening-up policy?

C: The Chinese economic reform and opening-up refers to the econmic overall plan of "Socialism with Chinese Characteristics" that was started by the Communist Party of China and led by Deng Xiaoping in December 1978.

F: Then what did China's economy look like before the reform?

C: The economic performance of China was poor in comparison with other East Asian economies. The economy was riddled with huge inefficiencies and malinvestment. One study noted that average level of pay in the catering sector exceeded that of intellectuals working in higher education.

F: That is terrible.

C: These eventful days, from December 18 to 22 in 1978, witnessed the meeting of delegates in Beijing for the Third Plenary Session of the 11th Central Committee of the Communist Party of China. So important was the decision made in the Great Hall of People and so far-reaching was its influence.

Micro-video

Reform in Agriculture

The theme of the plenary session in 1978 was emancipation of mind and transformation of the national focus to economic development. The reform and opening-up policy was first proposed in this session. Specifically, the term "reform and opening-up" refers to two important policy areas: internal reforms of China and the active external opening-up to the rest of the world. The reforms at home were intended to change the economic system and other factors that impeded the development of China's productivity in the past.

F: I can imagine that the country which was largely sealed off all the time has begun to open up cautiously to the outside world and to introduce important reforms slowly at home.

C: Yes. The first reform presided over by Deng began in agriculture, an industry with a long history of mis-management. Then, reforms were also implemented in urban industry to increase productivity. Deng created a series of special economic zones to attract foreign investment, which enjoy more open and flexible preferential policy and thus become engines of national economic growth.

F: That would be followed by economic growth for sure.

C: China has been widely seen as an engine of economic growth of countries and regions around the world. China's trade deficit with the rest of East Asia helps to revive the economy of Japan and Southeast Asia. Asian leaders view China's economic growth as an "engine of growth for all Asian countries."

F: It seems that it is not just economic growth...

C: With the policy of reform and opening-up, China has freed itself from poverty and stagnation and transformed itself into a society full of vigor and vitality. Today, anyone who walks through the streets and squares of Chinese cities and villages will be amazed by the colorful and cheerful life of Chinese people. The implementation of the reform and opening-up policy has revived the Chinese society and restored people's self-confidence and a sense of pride with the growing economic and political success. Now, a very cosmopolitan and diverse society has developed in China. The prosperity and diversity in Chinese culture today was unimaginable a few decades ago.

F: Through many years of reform and opening-up, one thing gets very clear: It is not only the Chinese people who benefit from the successful implementation of Deng's policy, but the people from the whole world.

C: According to Xi Jinping, China stands at a new historical starting point today. This is a starting point for China to develop a comprehensively deepening reform, to continuously push forward the economic and social development to adjust to new normal by transforming development mode. This is a new point for China to have an in-depth interaction and be deeply open to the world.

F: Definitely you will have a better China and we will have a better world.

中国的改革开放

（F:留学生　C:中国教授）

F:来到中国，我们看到的是一个积极进取、充满活力、发展迅速的国家，其经济实力已达到全球标准。一些中国的尖端技术正在逐渐占领世界市场，中国的消费品已经成为世界购物中心不可或缺的一部分，中国游客也主导着旅游业。我父亲20年前来过这里，在我来中国之前他跟我讲的是一个截然不同的中国。

C:如今看起来很自然的事情，在不久前还很难想象。

F:为什么？

C:中国今天的繁荣很大程度上归功于改革开放政策。

F:什么是改革开放？

C:中国的经济改革开放，是指1978年12月由邓小平主持、中国共产党领导的"中国特色社会主义"全面经济改革计划。

F:那么改革之前在中国经济如何呢？

C:与其他东亚经济体相比，中国的经济表现很差。当时经济上充斥着低效率和不良投资。一项研究指出，餐饮业的平均工资水平超过了从事高等教育的知识分子的工资水平。

F:确实糟糕。

C:1978年12月18日至12月22日举行了中国共产党第十一届中央委员会第三次全体会议。此次在人民大会堂里做出的决定至关重要，影响非常深远。

1978年全体会议的中心主题是解放思想，把国家的重点转移到经济建设上来。改革开放政策是在本届会议上首次提出的。具体来说，"改革开放"一词指的是两个重要的政策领域：对内改革和对外开放。对内改革旨在改变经济体制和其他过去阻碍中国生产力发展的因素。

F:我可以想象，那个曾一度封闭自守的国家这些年开始谨慎地对外开放，并在国内缓慢地推行重要的改革。

C:对的。邓小平主导的第一次改革始于农业，这是一个长期管理不善的产业。然后，城市工业也实施了改革以提高生产力。邓小平为引进外国投资创建了一系列经济特区，这些经济特区因为享受更加开放灵活的优惠政策，成为国民经济增长的引擎。

F:接下来经济肯定会增长。

C:中国已经被广泛视为全世界国家和地区经济增长的引擎。中国对东亚其他国家和地区的贸易逆差，帮助了日本和东南亚经济的复苏。亚洲领导人将中国的经济增长视为"亚洲所有国家的增长引擎"。

F:看来不仅仅是经济增长……

C:中国实行改革开放后,摆脱了贫困和停滞,建成了一个充满生机和活力的社会。今天,任何一个走过中国城市和村庄的街道以及广场的人都会为中国人民丰富多彩的生活感到惊奇。随着改革开放政策的实施,中国社会恢复了生机,人们恢复了自信心和自豪感。现在,一个非常国际化和多元化的社会已经在中国建设起来了。今天中国文化的繁荣和多样性,在几十年前是不可想象的。

F:经过多年的改革开放,有一件事是非常明确的:不仅是中国人民从邓小平政策的成功实施中受益,而且全世界人民都受益。

C:习近平指出,今天的中国,已经站在新的历史起点上。这个新起点,就是中国全面深化改革、增加经济社会发展新动力的新起点,就是中国适应经济发展新常态、转变经济发展方式的新起点,就是中国同世界深度互动、向世界深度开放的新起点。

F:你们一定会有一个更好的中国,我们也会有一个更美好的世界。

Exercise

Decide whether the following statements are TRUE or FALSE.

1. When coming to China, the foreign student sees the same view in China just as his father did 20 years ago.

2. China's reform and opening-up policy has lasted about 40 years.

3. The Chinese economic reform and opening-up policy was started in December 1978 by reformists within the Communist Party of China, led by Xi Jinping.

4. Actually before the reform, the average level of pay in the catering sector once exceeded that of intellectuals working in higher education.

5. The term "reform and opening-up" refers to two important policy areas: internal reforms within China itself and the active external opening-up to the rest of the world.

6. The reform began in big cities.

7. A series of special economic zones to attract foreign investment that was relatively free of the administrative regulations and interventions that hampered economic growth were created in the opening-up.

8. As a result of the reform and opening-up policy, only economic grows.

9. Chinese people are very confident about their future.

◎ *Text B*

China Ten Years Ago and Now Through the Eyes of Four Foreigners

1. Frau Ana from Germany, a designer, said, "Ten years ago the foreigner had a big car and a driver, and the Chinese would ride a bicycle or take the bus. Today? If you drive around downtown, you can see a switch in that..."

(How do you evaluate your experience in China?)

"The best decision I've ever made was moving here. It not only makes me follow my dreams professionally, but also shows me how close friendships can grow."

2. Pier Giraudi, a CEO from Italy, said, "Ten years ago life was much cheaper, with limited selection though. There is a big difference also among Chinese people, compared to the past. Now everything and everybody have become more international, more open...

Micro-video

Nobel Prize Winners' Talk

(How do you evaluate your experience in China?)

I like my life in China, I have a good experience. I feel Shanghai is my home and I'm not thinking about leaving. I've never had a breakdown. I enjoy all my time here."

3. Costas from Britain, said, "For the past 40 years, China has made remarkable achievements in economic development. China's development trend will continue, and its development prospect is bright. As far as China's domestic market is concerned, China will remain economically active and its import and export business is in good shape."

4. Now the Chinese economy is among the best in the world, according to Zuhal from Germany. Some argue that Europe and the US are leading the economy, but he thinks it could be ture 20 years ago, and that China's development is even more remarkable now.

He also thinks that the Chinese economy is expected to become the world's largest in the next 20 years. China is developing rapidly in the field of science and technology, such as mobile phones and unmanned aerial vehicles. China is transforming from "made in China" to "created in China," which is a great step forward.

四个外国人眼里10年前的中国和现在的中国

1. 来自德国的安娜夫人是一位设计师,她说:"10年前的外国人出门会有私家车跟司机,而中国人出门都是骑自行车或搭公交车,现在你到市中心看一下,情况完全是反过来的。"

(你如何评价在中国的这段经历?)

"来到中国是我人生中最美好的决定,不仅仅是让我追寻我的职业梦想,也让我见识到友情可以有多亲密。"

2. 来自意大利的某首席执行官皮尔·吉劳迪说:"10年前生活成本低很多,虽然选择也有限。与过去相比,中国人的变化也很大。现在中国人更为国际化,也更开放。"

(你如何评价在中国的这段经历?)

"我很喜欢在中国的生活,我有很美好的经历。我觉得上海就是我的家,我一点都不想离开。我一直过得很顺利,很享受在这里的时光。"

3. 来自英国的科斯塔斯表示:"过去40年来,中国在经济发展上取得了令人瞩目的成就。中国的发展态势仍将持续下去,发展前景一片光明。就中国国内市场来看,中国仍将保持经济活力,进出口业务态势良好。"

4. 来自德国的祖哈称,如今中国的经济位列世界前茅。有人认为欧美国家经济地位领先,但他认为那可能是20年前的事,如今中国的发展更加令世界瞩目。

祖哈认为未来20年,中国经济有望成为世界第一。中国在科技领域发展迅速,例如手机、无人机等产品。中国正在从"中国制造"转型为"中国创造",这是伟大的进步。

Exercises

Ⅰ *Answer the following questions after reading the text.*

1. What's your impression of China now?

2. If you can have a reform in China, which areas will you reform? How?

Ⅱ *Match the items in Column A with the items in Column B.*

Column A	Column B
1. 进出口业务	created in China
2. 国际化	opening-up
3. 中国创造	reform
4. 开放	international

5. 改革　　　　　　　import and export business

Chinese Eyes on the World

Frequent Stimulus Measures Have Not Worked

(C: Chinese student　J: Japanese student)

C: Every country will reform itself because of some problems in its own country. I think Japan is no exception.

J: Yes. Japan, for example, has undergone many reforms before it faces the growing problem of "advanced age with fewer children."

C: Advanced age with fewer children?

J: The so-called "advanced age with fewer children" refers to the declining birth rate and the increasing number of elderly people. This has developed into a serious problem in the Japanese society.

C: What about the government's reform measures?

J: Japan has taken a number of steps in response to concerns about the "advanced age with fewer children."

Beginning in 1995, the system of parental leave was established to spread the care and leave system for sick and injured children, and enhance health care for infants and pregnant women.

Japan's public spending on children has increased nearly every year since the 1990s, but the birth rate has continued to fall. Starting on April 1, 2010, Japan also began distributing child subsidies, and the guardians of children under the age of 15 can receive a child care subsidy of 13,000 yen per month.

Japan also has a number of laws relating to the promotion of fertility.

C: So many measures! That should be effective.

J: But the effect is not obvious. There are several reasons for this.

First of all, the values of young people are diversified, while the various mechanisms, institutions, and concepts of social life have not changed with them. Second, although the unemployment rate is not high, the income is too low for the young people to get married and have children, and child care subsidies may reduce family burden up to a point, but not enough to encourage marriage and child-bearing. Meanwhile, Japanese pensions are a mess, and young people are pessimistic about that. In addition, the Japanese economy is depressed, therefore, many people only have the nominal return to work after maternity leave because there is no actual position for them.

C: Although Japan has subsidized the fertility since 1972, the effect is not obvious. Japan's serious population problem is also a wake-up call for China.

Cultural Exchange

Ⅰ *Please discuss the following question in your group.*

Are there any reforms in your country? Please describe one in details.

Ⅱ *Give a reform plan for your country.*

Suppose you were the education minister of your country. Make a reform plan for the education of your country.

Extended Reading

Lee Kuan Yew, the Founding Father of Singapore

Chapter 16 Rural and Urban China

Text Reading

Micro-video

Rurual and Urban China

◎ *Text A*

The New Rural China

(C: Chinese　F: Foreigner)

C: Hi, Bill. How about your May Day Holiday?

F: Fantastic. We have been to Xiangshan. Wow, we didn't expect that Chinese countryside is so rich, clean, and beautiful. It is amazing.

C: That is true. Nowadays, when a holiday is coming, people in cities will rush to the countryside to enjoy the beautiful rural scenery. Even foreigners like you always marvel at the beauty of the Chinese countryside.

F: But I was told that Chinese countryside was very poor before I came to China.

C: That was also true. Chinese agricultural performance was extremely poor and food shortages were common before the Reform and Opening-up. Statistics show that after Deng Xiaoping implemented the rural household contract responsibility system, the total grain output of the country reached a new level one after another and the people's focus has shifted from how to have enough to eat to how to eat well. Farmers' income keeps growing. In 2017, the per capita disposable income of

rural residents reached 13,432 yuan, an average annual increase of 8.0% over the past five years. Accordingly the income gap between urban and rural residents is narrowing.

F: Mr. Deng Xiaoping is a great leader.

C: Yes. A more fundamental transformation was the economy's growing adoption of cash crops instead of just growing rice and grain. Vegetable and meat production increased to the point that Chinese agricultural production was adding the equivalent of California's vegetable industry every two years. Growth in the sector slowed after 1984, with agriculture falling from 40% of GDP to 16%; however, increases in agricultural productivity allowed workers to be released for work in industry and services, while simultaneously increasing agricultural production. Trade in agriculture was also liberalized and China became an exporter of food, a great contrast to its previous famines and shortages.

F: That is not a easy task.

C: China has also achieved "decisive progress" in the battle against poverty with more than 66 million people lifted out of poverty in the past five years (2012–2017).

F: But only being the winner in the battle against poverty is not enough for today's beautiful countryside.

C: You are right. Despite this progress a development gap remains between urban and rural regions principally due to lack of quality and efficiency in agriculture. Then, China has outlined tasks and targets for a rural vitalization strategy addressing issues related to agriculture, rural areas, and farmers.

F: No wonder it is reported that urban migrant workers return home to the countryside.

C: In 2017, Chinese government has proposed Rural Revitalization Strategy—that agriculture and rural areas must be prioritized in choosing cadres, the allocation of resources, public financial support, and public services. The strategy calls for the advance of integrated urban-rural development, with more focus on infrastructure, education, and public services in rural areas. The basic rural operation system should be consolidated and improved, while supply-side structural reform in rural areas should continue. And green development and innovative governance in rural areas will generate more sustained growth.

F: Then I am looking forward a more beautiful countryside.

C: Absolutely. By 2035, China aims for "decisive" progress, with basic modernization of agriculture and rural areas. By 2050, rural areas should have strong agriculture, a beautiful countryside, and well-off farmers.

中国新农村

（C：中国人　F：外国人）

C：嗨，比尔，你的五一假期过得怎样？

F：太棒了。我们去象山了。真没想到中国的农村如此富裕、整洁又美丽，令人惊叹。

C：的确如此。现在，每逢节假日，城市里的人们会涌向乡村，欣赏美丽的乡村风光。即使是你们外国人也总会惊叹中国农村的美丽。

F：但是在我来中国之前，有人告诉我中国农村很穷。

C：曾经的确如此。在改革开放前，中国的农业确实很弱，食物短缺的情况很普遍。统计数据表明，在邓小平实行农村家庭联产承包责任制后，全国粮食总产量接连跨上新台阶，确保了国家粮食安全，吃不饱饭彻底成为历史。农民收入不断增长，2017年农村居民人均可支配收入13432元，5年间年平均增长8.0%。城乡居民收入差距越来越小。

F：邓小平是一位伟大的领导人。

C：是的。经济上一个更根本的转变是越来越多地采用经济作物，而不是只种植大米和谷物。蔬菜和肉类产量的增加使得中国农产品产量增加了相当于加利福尼亚州蔬菜产业每两年的产量水平。1984年之后，农业增长放缓，农业从占GDP的40%下降到16%；然而，农业生产率的提高在增加农业生产的同时，使劳动力得以释放到工业和服务业。农业贸易自由化，中国成为食品出口国，这与之前的饥荒和食物短缺形成了鲜明的对比。

F：太不容易了。

C：中国在脱贫斗争中也取得了“决定性的进展”，在过去的五年里（2012—2017），有6600多万人摆脱了贫困。

F：如果仅仅是脱贫斗争的胜利，对今天的美丽乡村来说还是不够的。

C：没错。尽管农村发生了巨变，由于农业的质量和效率低下，城市和农村之间的发展差距仍然存在。所以后来中国提出了乡村振兴战略的任务和目标，解决了与农业、农村和农民有关的问题。

F：难怪据报道很多进城务工人员都回农村老家了。

C：2017年，中国政府提出了乡村振兴战略，指出要坚持农业农村优先发展，在干部配备上优先考虑，在要素配置上优先满足，在公共财政投入上优先保障，在公共服务上优先安排。呼吁推进城乡一体化发展，重点加强农村基础设施建设、教育事业发展和公共服务均等化。要巩固和完善农村基本经营制度，深化农村供给侧结构性改革。绿色发展和新农村治理体系创新将促进经济持续增长。

F：那我期待着一个更美丽的乡村。

C：当然。中国的目标是，到2035年乡村振兴取得决定性进展，农业农村现代化基本实现。到2050年，乡村全面振兴，农业强、农村美、农民富全面实现。

Exercises

Ⅰ *Answer the following questions based on what you have read in Text A.*

1. What is the new rural China like?
2. What was it like in the past?
3. What is the future of the new rural China?

Ⅱ *Match the items in Column A with the items in Column B.*

Column A	Column B
1. rural areas	洁净的
2. agriculture	贫穷的
3. beautiful	富裕的农民
4. well-off farmers	富裕的
5. rich	美丽的
6. clean	农业
7. poor	农村

◎ *Text B*

Shanghai and Chengdu

(F：Foreigner　C：Chinese)

Micro-video

Shanghai— City of Innovation

F：There are many cities in China. The most fashionable one is Shanghai, isn't it?

C：Yes, it is. Many westerners like Shanghai because of its cosmopolitan atmosphere. Shanghai people are smart and pragmatic. They are business-minded and have a high standard of ethics. For example, you seldom hear people accuse Shanghai taxi drivers of cheating. If you ask Shanghai people for directions, they will show you the most efficient route to your destination.

F：I was told that some MNC (multi-national corporation) employees in Shanghai prefer speaking English to Chinese in Shanghai.

C: I'm not surprised that this could happen in Shanghai. Shanghai has been heavily influenced by Western culture since the 1920s and 1930s. It was called "a paradise for adventurers." A lot of Western companies opened offices there. New ideas were brought in, together with the arrival of foreign businessmen and others. Shanghai was swept over by important merchandise, foreign languages, and jobs in foreign-owned companies.

F: Maybe as result, Shanghai people are very open-minded and receptive to new things.

C: Yes. Many new things were initially introduced to China through Shanghai. In the 1920s, some Shanghai art schools were the first in the country to use human models. Shanghai was also the first city to have movies. In the late 1970s, Shanghai was again among the first cities to send students to study abroad. Shanghai made products such as watches, bicycles, and sewing machines and enjoyed a very favorable reputation throughout the country even during the years of central economic planning. This reputation still benefits Shanghai today.

F: No wonder that some people say Shanghai is more like New York.

C: People used to make that comment in the 1930s. In many ways, Shanghai does look like New York. It is not New York. It is a Chinese city no matter what, and it is trendy Shanghai.

F: Is Shanghai the representative of Chinese cities?

C: We can't say that. Each Chinese city has its own characteristics. Shanghai, on the other hand, is viewed as a city of fashions. Ever since the 1930s, when Shanghai was under the Western rule, it has always been in full front of fashion. People like to call Beijing a political city because it's the capital and there are lots of bureaucrats. Even taxi drivers talk politics. Guangdong is the center of the economy where business has the priority. Chengdu is a happy-go-lucky city...

F: A happy-go-lucky city? Do you know anything about Chengdu? Can you tell me some?

C: Chengdu is the capital city of Sichuan Province. The temperature is mild and the land is very productive, in fact, so fertile that it is said even a stick will grow. The favorable environment has given rise to a very easy and relaxed life style. Many Chengdu people drive a small fuel-efficient car called auto. The car didn't sell well in Beijing because people in Beijing thought it was too shabby. In fact, autos were even not allowed on Chang'an Avenue in Beijing for some time.

F: I remembered I was told that one beautiful city is known for its tea houses. Is it Chengdu?

C: Yes, there are tea houses everywhere. Unlike some other big cities, where tea houses are graded to serve different customers, tea houses in Chengdu offer a whole range of products. Everyone, yet a businessman, a migrant worker, or a student can find something they want. People can spend a whole day in the tea house, either to talk business or simply relax.

Micro-video

Chengdu City

F: Are there any other interesting games there?

C: Mahjong is a popular game among tea house goers in Chengdu. There was a joke on the Internet that says as soon as the plane enters the Chengdu airspace, passengers can hear the sound of mahjong shuffling.

Chengdu is also known for its snacks. There are plenty of columns in the newspaper and entertainment outlets on TV and radio. You don't always find a kind of restlessness in Chengdu as in other cities. But this doesn't mean Chengdu people have closed minds. On the contrary, they are very open-minded.

F: It's good for a person to be happy and forget about fame and wealth.

C: This reminds me of a Chinese saying, "A lucky person doesn't have to chase luck."

上海和成都

（C:中国人　F:外国人）

F:中国这么多城市里,最时尚的是上海,对吗?

C:是的。许多西方人喜欢国际大都市上海。上海人既聪明又务实。他们既有商业头脑,又有很高的道德标准。例如,你很少听到人们指责上海出租车司机有违规行为。如果你向上海人问路,他们会给你指出到达目的地的最短路线。

F:我听说上海的一些跨国公司员工喜欢说英语,而不说中文。

C:在上海有这样的现象,我并不感到惊讶。从20世纪二三十年代开始,上海就深受西方文化的影响。它被称为“冒险家的天堂”。许多西方的公司在那里开设了办事处。随着各国商人和其他人员的到来,新观念也随之产生。外国公司的重要商品、外语和外资企业的工作岗位席卷了整个上海。

F:也许这使得上海人非常开放,乐于接受新事物。

C:是的,许多新鲜事物最初是通过上海传入中国的。在20世纪20年代,一些上海的艺术学校是全国第一批使用人体模特的学校。上海也是第一个拥有电影院的城市。20世纪70年代末,上海又是首批送学生出国留学的城市。那时,上海生产手表、自行车、缝纫机等产品,即便是在计划经济年代,上海也是享誉全国。这样的声誉让上海受益至今。

F:难怪有人说上海像纽约。

C:在20世纪30年代,人们常常发表这样的评论。从很多方面来看,上海的确跟纽约很像,但它不是纽约。它是一个中国的城市,无论如何,它是时尚的上海。

F:上海是中国城市的代表吗?

C:不好这么说。中国的城市各有自己的特色。而上海则被视为一个时尚之都。20世纪30年代以来,上海深受西方的影响,一直处于时尚的前沿。人们喜欢称北京为政治城市,因为它是首都,那里有很多政府机构,甚至出租车司机也谈论政治。广东是经济至上的城市,在那里,商业有优先权。成都是一个休闲自在的城市……

F:休闲自在?你了解成都吗?你能和我说说吗?

C:成都是四川省的省会。气温适宜,土地肥沃,有人戏称此处土地肥沃到插一根棍子也会生长。良好的环境造就了一种轻松悠闲的生活方式。许多成都人开的一种小型节能车在北京卖得不好,因为北京人认为这种车太寒酸了。事实上,北京长安街甚至在一段时间内都不允许开这种车。

F:我记得有人告诉我,有一个美丽的城市以茶馆而闻名,那是成都吗?

C:是的,成都到处都有茶馆。与其他大城市为不同顾客提供不同服务的茶馆不同,成都的茶馆提供全系列的产品。每个人,无论商人、进城务工人员,还是学生都能找到他们想要的东西。人们可以在茶馆里待上一整天,或是谈生意,或是休闲放松。

F:茶馆里还有什么有趣的游戏吗?

C:麻将在成都的茶馆里很受欢迎。网上有个笑话说,飞机一进入成都上空,乘客就能听到搓麻将的声音。成都也以小吃闻名。报纸上有很多的美食专栏,电视和广播电台也有很多关于美食的娱乐节目。和其他城市一样,在成都,你也总能找到安定的感觉。但这并不意味着成都人的思想是封闭的。相反,他们的思想很开放。

F:这真是一个让人感到幸福的城市,在这里可以忘掉名利。

C:这让我想起了中国的一句谚语:“吉人自有天相。”

Exercises

Ⅰ *Fill in the chart with the features of these two cities.*

Shanghai	Chengdu

Ⅱ *Please translate the following words and phrases into Chinese.*

1. fashionable
2. Shanghai
3. fame and wealth
4. fertile
5. environment
6. relaxed
7. economic growth
8. the National Day golden week holidays
9. top ten

Chinese Eyes on the World

New York City

Micro-video

New York City

Among foreign cities, New York city is the earliest known to most Chinese and also a city that many Chinese yearn for.

The City of New York (NYC), located on the Atlantic coast of southeast New York, is the largest city and the largest port in the United States.

New York city is the heart of the New York metropolitan area, an international metropolis, and one of the world's largest economic centers. In 2017, New York's regional GDP has reached US $9, 007 billion, which directly affects the global financial, media, political, entertainment, and fashion sectors.

New York city is the most populous city in the US and a multi-ethnic city with over 800 languages spoken in 97 countries and regions. By 2014, there were about 8.49

million people in New York city, living on 789 square kilometers of land. The New York metropolitan area has around 20 million people.

New York city also wields enormous influence in business and finance. Its financial district, led by lower Manhattan and Wall Street, is known as the world's financial center, with 56 of the world's top 500 companies based there. The New York Stock Exchange, the world's second-largest stock exchange, was once the largest exchange, with a global market capitalization of US $15 trillion, until it was overtaken by Nasdaq in 1996. The New York Times Square, located at the Broadway theater district hub, is known as the "crossroads of the world" and is one of the centers of the world's entertainment industry. Manhattan's Chinatown is the densest concentration of Chinese in the western hemisphere.

The New York subway is one of the most developed fast transportation systems in the world, running 24 hours a day and seven days a week. New York city has Columbia University, New York University, and Rockefeller University.

New York city is a new place for immigrants and people think opportunities are everywhere. So New York city is often nicknamed the "Big Apple" for "it's good looking, tasty, and everyone wants to take a bite."

On September 11, 2001, at about 8:45 a.m., terrorists hijacked two commercial planes and crashed into the World Trade Center, causing major casualties and shocking the world.

Cultural Exchange

Ⅰ *Discuss the following questions with your peers.*

1. Which city in the world is your favorite? Can you tell us the reason?

2. Can you describe your hometown?

3. Are there any differences between Chinese cities/rural areas and the ones in your country?

Ⅱ *Fill in the blanks according to your knowledge.*

In the countryside, especially in a traditional, agricultural society there was almost no population mobility. People lived in one place for generations with no interaction with the 1. ______ world. Everyone knew everyone else, and this led to a lot of 2. ______ understanding and interdependence. At that time, neighbors seemed to be an important part of community relationship. Whenever someone needed any help, the first solution was to ask the 3. ______. This is where the expression, "A neighbor is more dependable than a 4. ______" came from.

For instance, if the neighbors heard a couple having a noisy fight, they would come over to 5. ______ them 6. ______. Or, if both the husband and the wife were working, they would give their house key to the woman next door so that she could help look after the children after school. The "bound feet security guards" was a very popular expression in the 20th century. It refers to the retired people, usually old woman, who would walk around their neighborhood to 7. ______.

Now especially in the cities, people live in high-rise apartment buildings, the 8. ______ that was typical in a traditional courtyard is gone. People live behind closed doors and often do not even know the 9. ______. The older people, in particular, have problems 10. ______ to this change. This is why you always see groups of old people socializing in public green areas. They miss the intimate community of their private life, and they also appreciate a friendly 11. ______.

Ⅲ *In this part there are five topics. Work in small groups and then talk about them in class.*

1. What is the most difficult thing you find in communicating with foreigners? How do you improve your communication skills?

2. Have you found any differences between Chinese culture and the culture of your country? Name some.

3. How does a culture influence the way its people speak?

4. What do you speak when you talk with your friends, the standard English/Chinese or the local dialect? Why?

5. Some foreigners say that Chinese is quite loose in grammar. Do you agree or disagree? Cite some examples to support your point of view.

References

陈莹. 国际汉语文化与文化教学[M]. 北京:高等教育出版社,2013.

崔刚,莫嘉琳. 中国传统文化英文入门教程[M]. 北京:清华大学出版社,2015.

崔喜哲. 每天读点英美文化[M]. 北京:中国水利水电出版社,2011.

董俊峰. 中国文化专论[M]. 杭州:浙江大学出版社,2011.

黄建滨. 中国文化英语阅读教程[M]. 上海:上海外语教育出版社,2013.

教育部课程教材研究所. 中国文化读本[M]. 北京:人民教育出版社,2007.

李霞. 趣读中国人[M]. 北京:外文出版社,2009.

李霞. 英语国际人:英语畅谈中国文化50主题[M]. 北京:外文出版社,2007.

廖华英. 跨文化交际案例分析[M]. 北京:北京理工大学出版社,2010.

刘和林. 跨文化交际实用英语教程[M]. 长沙:湖南大学出版社,2016.

龙江. 英语漫谈中国文化[M]. 大连:大连理工大学出版社,2010.

南寻. Taiji quan (shadow boxing)[EB/OL]. (2010-11-18) [2017-08-17]. http://blog.sina.com.cn/s/blog_6e993f180100mhus.html.

任勤,廖雷朝. 中美文化面面观[M]. 重庆:重庆大学出版社,2010.

孙若男. 在华老外眼中的中国改革开放:变化翻天覆地 国富民强引人羡慕[EB/OL]. (2018-03-28) [2018-04-30]. http://news.sina.com.cn/gov/2018-03-28/doc-ifysqfnh9498824.shtml.

微萌. 边学英语边品中国文化[M]. 北京:中国时代经济出版社,2011.

杨枫. 朗文文化交际英语[M]. 长春:吉林出版集团有限公司,2006.

赵金磊. Values and Beliefs[EB/OL]. (2010-09-16) [2017-09-10]. http://blog.sina.com.cn/s/blog_6288d80f0100lul5.html.

ANON. Amazing facts you didn't know about the Terracotta Warriors[EB/OL]. [2017-06-28]. https://www.travelchinaguide.com/attraction/shaanxi/xian/terra_cotta_army/facts.htm.

ANON. China 10 years ago and now through the eyes of 5 foreigners[EB/OL].(2016-03-

25) [2017-09-15]. https://mp. weixin. qq. com / s? __biz=MjM5MjU0MzE3Nw% 3D% 3D&idx=1&mid=403502885&scene=21&sn=73191695c063a911ee686c4b9343f04f.

ANON. Chinese art: Chinese Qipao, cheongsam 旗袍[EB/OL]. (2013-15-02) [2017-06-19]. http://www.hjenglish.com/speeches/p477396/.

ANON. Chinese clothing[EB/OL]. [2017-06-16]. https://www.travelchinaguide.com/intro/clothing/.

ANON. Chinese values, customs and beliefs[EB/OL]. [2017-09-01]. http://www.lotustours.net/info/connect/culture/culture2.shtml.

ANON. Difference between Chinese and western medicine[EB/OL]. [2017-06-13]. http://www.differencebetween.net / science / health / difference-between -chinese-and-western -medicine/.

ANON. Eight cuisines of China—Fujian and Anhui[EB/OL]. [2017-06-28]. https://www.travelchinaguide.com/intro/cuisine_drink/cuisine/eight_cuisines3.htm.

ANON. Traditional Chinese medicine[EB/OL]. [2017-10-12]. https://www.chinahighlights.com/travelguide/culture/traditionalmedichine.htm.

ANON. What is the difference between Chinese medicine and western medicine? [EB/OL]. [2017-10-15]. http://www.wisegeek.com/what-is-the-difference-between-chinese-medicine-and-western-medicine.htm.

BERMAN J, E FRANCIS. What makes a family? children, say many Americans[EB/OL]. (2010-09-15) [2017-09-25]. http://abcnews. go. com / WN / defines-family - children - americans-survey/story? id=11644693.

China Flight Crew. Taiji shadow boxing[EB/OL]. (2014-07-11). [2017-08-17]. https://mp.weixin.qq.com/s? 3rd=MzA3MDU4NTYzMw%3D%3D&__biz=MjM5MjYzOTg2Mw%3D%3D&idx=3&mid=200815589&scene=6&sn=e47b6a6f67f9bfb5406748ef43e1f249.

DAMEN L. Culture learning: the fifth dimension in the language classroom [M]. Reading: Addison-Wesley, 1987.

DATESMAN M K. The American ways: an introduction to American culture[M]. Saddle River: Orentice Hall Regents, 1997.

HALL E T. The hidden dimension[M]. New York: Anchor Press/Doubleday, 1966.

HALL E T. Beyond culture[M]. Garden City: Double Day, 1977.

HOFSTEDE G. National cultures and corporate cultures [M]//L A SAMOVAR, R E PORTER. Communication between cultures. Belmont: Wadsworth, 1984.

STIRK N. 英语国际人:英语畅谈世界文化100主题[M]. 许卉艳,周维,译. 北京:外文出版社,2007.

TYLER E B. Primitive culture[M]. London: J. Murray, 1871.

YANG JINSONG. A successful warrior in Chinese films[N]. China daily, 2017-08-18.